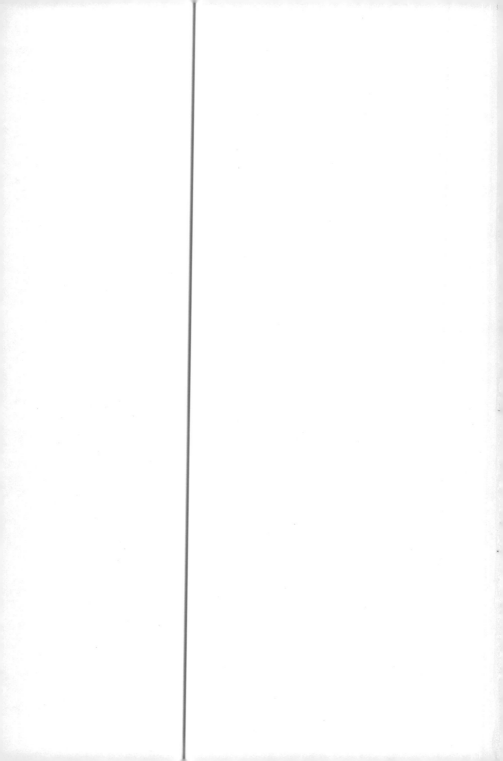

WHY I WORE
LIPSTICK
TO MY MASTECTOMY

"The FCC is launching an investigation into the nipple."
> —*Tom Preston, president of* MTV, *on Janet Jackson's breast baring performance at the Superbowl*

"I moved to the United States after seeing *Baywatch* on television."
> —*Sarabjeet Multani, a fast-driving, Punjabi, New York City cabbie*
> The New York Times, *July 17, 2003*

"I'm often taken aback by the phenomenon it's become—I just don't believe it sometimes."
> —*Joe Francis, founder of* Girls Gone Wild. *His teams of cameramen ask young women—in return for a* Girls Gone Wild *tank top—to sign a release form and reveal their naked breasts.*

"Silly little planet. I could rule the world with these mammary things."
> —*Lara Flynn Boyle as Serleena in* Men in Black 2, *upon landing on earth and causing chaos in her black push-up bra*

"People need to realize that breasts are for more than selling beer."
> —*Tristyn Underwood, nursing her twenty-eight-month-old son, Gabriel, at a "nurse-in" at a Utah Burger King to protest a woman being asked to nurse her baby in the bathroom instead of the playroom*

"The chain acknowledges that many consider 'Hooters' a slang term for a portion of the female anatomy. The chain enjoys and benefits from this debate."
> —*From the official Hooters restaurant Web site*

Geralyn Lucas

WHY I WORE LIPSTICK
TO MY MASTECTOMY

St. Martin's Press ✿ New York

www.stmartins.com

Design by Kathryn Parise

ISBN 0-312-33445-1
EAN 978-0312-33445-1

First Edition: October 2004

10 9 8 7 6 5 4 3 2 1

Note to Readers

Conversations quoted in this book have been reconstructed from memory.

While Geralyn is deeply grateful to all of her doctors for their amazing dedication, skill, and compassion; she has omitted their names out of respect for the doctor/patient relationship.

For Moni
By Christine Thomas

Gliding down the mountain
Soaring through the air
The snow it falls so steady
It's sprinkled in her hair

A young and vibrant woman
Slowly lost her strength
It seemed to me impossible
It seems so to this day

To have such grace and beauty
Inside as well as out
Was such an inspiration
And now I am without

This poem was written for Monica Steward, a beautiful young woman who had so much life left in her when she died of breast cancer. She was only twenty-eight years old.

I dedicate this book to all the women whose lives were stolen, and to all the families who lost them. There was so much more life left in all of them. I have cried for Stacey, for Laurel, for Amy, for Becky, for Julie, for Anne, for Erin, and for Monica.

I am convinced that it is not about "beating" breast cancer. It is not about positive attitude, eating the right food, exercise, whatever. They were all fighters, and if anyone could've "beaten" cancer, these women could have. They were totally kick-ass.

I don't know why I lived and others died. That is the worst part for me. I have survivor's guilt. But, I know their spirits, and the love for them lives on.

I also dedicate this book to the amazing doctors who put my boob and my life back together again, somehow: Thank you for the work you do every day. Thank you for your devotion to taking care of women and their families.

And, this dedication is also to all the survivors who have supported me. I am humbled by your courage, your strength, and generosity. Thank you Meredith, Rena, and Jane for all of your guidance and for being my touchstones. I am in awe of all the other one boobed girls, and no boobed girls, I have met who still know how to work it—you showed me a way and you know who you are! You have proven to me that breast cancer survivors are some of the smartest *and* foxiest women I know. It must be all of that inner cleavage shining through! You know how to strip. You go girls!

XO Geralyn

Contents

Contents ❦ xii

The Lipstick Manifesto: Have Courage, Wear Lipstick

Lipstick—I never used to wear it. I used to be strictly a gloss girl: Bonne Bell. Lipstick was reserved for movie stars, rocker chicks, magazine-ad models, and a certain type of woman that I knew I was not. It felt obvious and too bold and shouted *look at me!* I didn't have the self-confidence and couldn't pull it off.

I started slowly, with tinted gloss. When I put my finger in the round jar, it stained my fingertip slightly and it felt incriminating. It was in chemistry class in high school. I thought no one would notice there because of all the beakers, chemicals, and the potential for explosions. I checked my lips twice in the reflective paper towel holder when I washed my hands, and both times I was a little startled by how much my lips stood out. That kind of made me smirk. I think my teacher, Mr. Bradley, might have noticed this change because he looked at me funny—either that or he was scared I was going to ignite my notebook.

The tinted gloss sustained me until college, when I received some red lipstick as a free gift with a purchase. It was something I never would have bought, because it was too sexy for me.

I got a tissue ready just in case the lipstick looked ridiculous, closed my door, and locked it. I remembered I had watched in awe when other women confidently applied their lipstick in bathroom mirrors. Lips slightly puckered, every single stroke seemed to say, *I deserve this*. As I glided it across my lips my hand shook a little and I had to wipe it off and start again. Now I had a red smudge around my lips and I was worried my lipstick experiment might backfire and that I would look like a little girl playing dress-up—or Ronald McDonald.

When I looked in the mirror I was confused. I definitely didn't look like Marilyn Monroe, but there was something about myself I didn't recognize. Some sort of confidence was on my lips staring back at me, daring me to live up to this fierce red lipstick I had just applied.

Something changed when I put on that lipstick that day. It was like a magic wand when I swiped the waxes, oils, pigments, and emollients across my lips for the first time. But then I panicked and worried. Could I live up to my lipstick? Could I own this new power?

Now, applying lipstick is a habit, like brushing my teeth. I even amped it up. I prefer bright red. It has become my trademark. When women compliment my lipstick they almost always say, "Oh, I could never wear red lipstick, but it looks so good on you."

I always think to myself: "You *can* wear lipstick . . . you've never tried."

And maybe applying red lipstick is a simple act of courage—to imagine yourself as someone or something you never thought you could be, and somehow, in a carefully applied swipe of beeswax, to become her.

Maybe wearing lipstick is the beginning of a revolution inside your head?

1

Stripping

I am the only woman in the room with my shirt on at the VIP Strip
Club (except for the coat-check girl and she definitely doesn't
count). So I am trying to blend in but it is not working. A preppy
guy has already come over and asked if I would spank him. One of
the bouncers heard this and moved me over to a more private corner of the club. I appreciate this gesture because I have come here
to face the biggest decision of my life, and the disco music was just
too loud in the front to really concentrate.

I have never been in a strip club before, and they would not allow me in without a man. It was more humiliating than being
carded. So I waited for the next guy to show up and asked if he

would be my escort. At first I was embarrassed, but then I got over it because I need to be here.

I have come to this mammary Mecca to decide if I can decide to have a mastectomy to deal with the cancer they found in my right breast ten days ago. This was one part of the diagnosis that no one would discuss with me: what it means to have one boob in a boob-obsessed universe. It seems taboo to actually admit this, or to factor it into my decision about whether I should have a mastectomy. But for me, it is now, strangely, the deciding factor. The argument for having the mastectomy and removing my breast seems pretty obvi-ous—it would be so much safer—until I start thinking about how I will exist as a twenty-seven-year-old woman with one breast. I am not a stripper, but I have always taken for granted that I have two boobs.

I am scared that admitting that this is my wild card will make me a shallow person. I mean, we are talking about cancer here. So I am here at the strip club to confront the unspeakable.

Breasts are beautiful, I agree as I plop into my plush purple vel-vet chair. The view is much better from back here. It is sort of pretty—the room is sprinkled with shimmers from the huge mir-rored disco ball swirling overhead. There is purple velvet on the walls and even on the floor. I catch my reflection in the smoky mir-rors, and I am illuminated by strange lighting that is dimmed, but more fluorescent than romantic. There is a stage with purple cur-tains and the disco ball hangs directly above where each dancer stands when she's announced by a deejay in a booth off stage. The carpeting precisely matches the purple velvet chairs (which I have noticed, if you stare too closely, have stains). Cocktails, cigarette ashes, and maybe some other nasty stuff. I think that's why they picked deep purple—it hides stains and wear and tear. Yes, this is a high-volume place. Lots of breasts, lots of guys, and lots of noise. I can smell sex in the air, and it smells like a locker room after a football game, covered in aftershave.

All the men in this room are reminding me of the power I stand to lose. They are here to worship boobs. I don't think that I'm being masochistic, sitting in a strip club looking at beautiful breasts before my breast surgery. It is a fact everyone has been ducking: Boobs matter. A breast is somehow more than flesh and blood. Everywhere in life, but especially here. This is a crash course, a CliffsNotes on why boobs matter so much. Men are paying a lot of money to look. And acting really stupid. Let's face it—they would not be behaving this way if the women were on stage pulling down their socks to reveal their ankles. What is it about boobs?

The cocktail waitress takes my drink order, a Budweiser in the bottle, no glass, because I need to look a little tough sitting in the strip club. I start the pep talk to myself that I have formulated since my diagnosis: It's pure biology. Breasts feed us when we are babies and it is hard-wired into us to like them, look at them, and covet them. Breasts symbolize a woman's fertility, so it is all part of our mating dance.

Somehow this doesn't make me feel better. Actually, I feel worse. I want to be something men are hard-wired to respond to. I still look young enough to get carded, and I want to be fertile, healthy, and hopefully, able to feed a baby someday.

But then the other pep talk: Why does my boob matter? At least it's my right boob and not my right hand. If it were my right hand, then I couldn't write. I have done just fine keeping my shirt on, thank you. After all, I'm only a 32 A, it's not like my boobs have caused any major distractions. I will probably keep my job at ABC News *20/20*, my husband, Tyler, and my friends with just one. Tyler is a doctor, so he can probably handle a medical condition. Besides, he's not a breast man—he even had his bachelor party in a steak house, not a strip bar. But that was before we knew that I would only have one boob. Now would he need to come to a place like this to look at two?

I pay a boob-inflated price for my nine-dollar Bud, and I finally allow myself to look. And I can't help but stare. I have the prop of the beer bottle now, so I can finally even cry a little and hide behind it. I don't want to ogle, but I can't help myself.

Boobs—lots of them. I can't describe my longing. There is every model here: big, small, firm, giggly, *Baywatch*-fake, and yet they are all somehow perfect. The symmetry is what strikes me most—the pairs—like ears, like knees, like eyes, like feet. They are two that go together.

I am daring myself to keep staring at boobs and that is when I see her.

"Gentlemen!" the deejay is in his booth, but his voice is booming.

"The lovely, *loveely, loveeeely*—Erica!"

She is on stage to take her turn, to dance her number under the disco ball. I notice her face first and not her boobs. She has this smirk in her eyes, and even though she is taking off her sequined top for strange men on a stage with strobe lights flashing on her nipples, she seems sort of . . . modest? Like she is holding on to a piece of herself that she will not just give away. So many of the other dancers here look cheesy, like a cartoon version of sexy. Some of them look vacant, like they are looking past these ogling men, looking somewhere far away. But she, she is so fiery. She is totally absorbed in the music and I really think she is just dancing for herself. And somehow it is not about her boobs really—it feels so much bigger than that.

Oops. She definitely caught me checking her out on the stage and I think I am turning bright red. I'm trying to dab my cheeks and trying to wipe my mascara smears with my palms to hide the fact that I have been crying. She finishes her dance, comes off the stage, and walks towards the back of the club right over to me.

"Can I cheer you up?"

She must think I had a really bad break-up with a girlfriend. She straddles me and starts to push her perfect mounds of cancer-free flesh into my face, and all I can think about is how beautiful her nipples are, and how I need to cut one of mine off to save my life. I am trying to play along and be cool, but I have never had a lap dance and now that she is pushing her breasts against me it is making me sad and envious. I don't even care that there are guys staring at us now. I am no longer self-conscious about being a woman sitting in a strip club. I have joined the guys and I am in a booby trance.

There is something about her and the way she has stripped in front of me. She is holding on so tightly to herself that maybe she is sending me a message? It is like she is telling me to hold on tight and not give it all away. She finally finishes and I notice her swagger as she walks away.

I cool down, order another Bud, and start to refocus on my agenda. I remember what I said to every male breast surgeon during my appointments: "My breasts mean nothing to me. I studied hard my whole life. I did not get where I am because of my breasts. I will cut them off to save my life. Please tell me the truth."

My dad was the one who flagged it. "The lady doth protest too much." His probing green eyes were telling me to go deeper. I was just intrigued that Shakespeare could hold a key to my boob dilemma. "Of course your breast means something to you, sweetie."

Both my parents are therapists so it figures that I am avoidant.

But I know why I need to use the blatant disclaimer that my boobs don't matter. The six male surgeons I have had consults with about my case can't look me in the eyes. I have long hair, I wear lipstick, and I know what they are thinking. In fact one of them just said it out loud: "It would be so unfortunate to lose your breast. You're such an attractive young woman."

The closest the other five male doctors come to speaking the unspeakable is to tell me the lumpectomy would be easier, it would leave me more "unchanged." It would leave me with only a small scar—they would have a plastic surgeon come in and stitch me up. So the wild card is there: What would it mean for me to have a mastectomy and lose my breast and a nipple? The nipple part really bothers me. And at the VIP Strip Club all I am thinking is that I could never work here without a nipple. Well, maybe I could be part of a freak show or fetish show or something. But 99.9 percent of men would not pay me to take my shirt off.

Wait! This is ridiculous! I've never even wanted to be a stripper! But now it is really bothering me that I can't do it. I don't even want to, but I can't.

Things are getting really rowdy at the VIP Strip Club. There are cheers at the next table and lots of high fives, and it is all about boobs. There is such desire in their eyes and in their hearts, and at this point they are all hypnotized.

That's when I slowly start to feel the power in this room building force, but draining out of me. Like the water draining from a bathtub, the suction is gathering strength, and I finally understand what is ahead.

Just the way some of the women doctors look me in the eye without even blinking and insist I have my breast removed. In fact, one recommends having both my breasts removed. They are sort of cruel in the way they tell me and seem uncomfortable when I cry. It is as if their faces are saying, "You have a lot more to cry about than just losing your breast . . . you might die." They don't want to acknowledge the wild card. Maybe it is easier for them because they each have two breasts that no one is telling them to cut off.

Halfway through my third Bud, the beer is settling in and I have a buzz and I am pretty sure that somehow I can face having a mastectomy instead of a lumpectomy. Because I would never forgive myself if the cancer returned. That, with an open heart and three Buds, feels like the easy part. The harder part is what is happening in this room. Why boobs rule men. Why boobs are a commodity. Why a boob is not an elbow. Why there are such things as strip clubs, where men pay women to see their breasts. That part is as much about my survival as my prognosis. But no one has said that to me—I just know it.

It is a strange place to finally say good-bye to my right boob, but this whole situation is so fucking uncharted.

I remember my first training bra and how the hook never stayed closed.

I remember going to second base in the stairwell after junior prom with Flip.

I remember my first red-and-white bikini and how daring I felt when Patrick untied the top so I wouldn't get a tan line on my back.

I remember when all the girls came back from summer vacation after seventh grade with boobs and I was still waiting.

I remember that I was always the smart girl.

I remember when boobs were not my best feature, clearly not what defined me.

I remember when my breasts were not something that could kill me.

Now I want more. I want the power in this room. I want to have what they have. Now that I'm losing that feature, I am concerned that it mattered more than I thought.

It is just too deep and complicated for me to figure out right this minute, especially with Donna Summer's "Bad Girls" blaring in the background. I know my husband will probably go to strip clubs with his orthopedic surgeon colleagues at conventions. I will sit at home with one boob, thinking of him looking at perfect boobs. Will my brother Paul plan our brother Howard's bachelor party in a strip club? I look around the smoky VIP Strip Club and I see brothers, husbands, dads, friends, bosses, all leering, and maybe because I am drunk I will admit that I am jealous and want to know they would leer at me, too, even after my surgery.

I leave forty dollars on a twenty-seven dollar tab because I am too embarrassed to ask for change. I stand up to leave the club. I walk past the breasts on parade, past the commotion, and past the testosterone.

The bouncer smiles at me when he holds open the door and I feel a small victory. Because I caught his eye with my smile. There's a ratty maroon velvet rope outside to cordon off the entrance to the club. I am leaving the world of boobs.

As I hail a taxi at the corner, I start to think about how the excitement in that room did not begin until the tops came off. I have kept my shirt on until now (well, most of the time) and still gotten paid, gotten loved, and gotten noticed. When I lose my breast I will be stripped of part of what I thought made me a woman, made me desirable. But, I think, I will still be me.

Maybe I am like an antique table that is being stripped before being re-varnished. Layers will be peeled away to reveal something beautiful underneath. Actually, maybe the ultimate striptease is ahead of me: First my breast will be cut off. Then my hair will fall out. And when there is nothing left to strip, maybe there will be a revelation of a different beauty underneath, one that I never knew existed.

I will be stripped to the core but I will still be there.

I think of myself on that stage with the strobe light on me: it is the striptease of my life.

I will find a way to exist.

Somehow.

2

Lumps

I knew it was bad news.

Two men in white coats. Both of them crying.

I was in a windowless white room with a tacky nature print on the wall and it felt like the scene in a movie where the woman finds out that she has cancer and she will die young. But it was real.

My husband's white coat says "Dr. Lucas" across his chest in happy cursive. Maybe Tom Cruise would play Tyler? It is a total stretch, but Tyler is handsome and has amazing blue eyes and fabulous shoulders. He looks like a doctor on a soap opera, but he really went to medical school. But I know that medical school hasn't prepared him for being thirty-two, married only two years, and finding out that his wife has breast cancer.

The other white coat belongs to my breast surgeon, Dr. B. He had predicted it would never be cancer because I was only twenty-seven, because I had no family history, because I looked so healthy. Bruce Willis or another sexy balding actor would play him. He looks exactly like what a doctor looks like in the movies when there is bad news. But his tears are real. He looks at me and finally says it.

"You do have cancer"—pause—"but we will cure you."

Strange, I have never heard the words "cancer" and "cure" in the same sentence before. Is he lying to me?

I understand why Tyler is crying. I know that we said in sickness and in health, but there has got to be some sort of exit clause when something like this happens. Dr. B, I understand his tears, too. He probably has done this scene hundreds of times in his office. I wonder if delivering bad news got easier after some practice. Clearly, he is not immune to it. But there is an extra level of bad news here. I am his colleague's wife. It is personal.

Now, if two grown men, doctors, cannot handle this information, how am I supposed to? But somehow I hear myself rally like I always do. I should not have been cut from the seventh-grade cheerleading team. I do not cry.

"It will be okay," I am trying to convince the doctors. "I'll be fine." That last sentence hangs in the air, and they both look at me like I don't get it. Like, "Oh, we just told her that she has cancer and she's in denial." I am not in denial. I am scared, though.

I realize in that small windowless office that this is about having no control. This is something that just happened. So, if I didn't cause this, how can I fix it? My body has betrayed me. How can I count on it to get better? To fix itself? I have always been a good "fixer." I am the one my parents call to tell my younger brothers what to do. I instruct my friends about how to break up with their boyfriends. Now I see that this might be unfixable.

"Do I need to have chemotherapy, will I lose my hair?"

I am so embarrassed that the only lame thing I can think about is whether my hair will fall out. I must seem so vain, but I have always pictured cancer patients with bald heads.

Dr. B tells me that it is too early to make that decision, that we will have the full pathology report back tomorrow and I will need to consult an oncologist.

I am not prepared for this scene to unfold in my life. I never had a biopsy. The word *biopsy* even sounds serious. I never even had my tonsils out, or broke my arm. I ate a cheeseburger before my biopsy and I saw white dots when Dr. B was cutting into my breast to get to that lump. During the biopsy I could still taste the ketchup in my mouth even though the smell of alcohol was so heavy in the room.

I knew when I first felt the lump in the shower that it felt like trouble. My fingertips just knew it was bad news. I should not have been worried because my mom and grandmothers had never had breast cancer. But I was worried. I was dripping wet, still in my towel when I told Tyler about the lumps. There were actually three of them.

"Geralyn, you're being a hypochondriac. Just because you found a lump you think you have breast cancer? Women always have lumps. It's nothing."

Tyler was annoyed with me—I could tell by his tone of voice.

I didn't understand why he was so annoyed, considering he was the one who had taught me how to do a breast self-exam in the first place. When I first met Tyler, he was doing a rotation as the breast resident. Aside from it being especially intimidating to show him my breasts, it affected me to hear him so devastated by what he had seen. On our first date he told me all about the young mother with breast cancer he had just done a mastectomy on. She was only twenty-eight and he thought she was going to die. He couldn't believe how many women, especially young women, had breast cancer. He made me learn how to do a breast self-exam. He had told me that one of my friends, someone I knew, would get breast cancer—it was pure statistics.

We both never imagined that the woman who would get breast cancer would be me. Meeting Tyler would save my life.

But now that I had actually done the breast exam and I had found lumps, he didn't seem concerned. He seemed more upset that we were late to a movie, because I was always late. He was always on time. Maybe he was snapping at me because he, too, was terrified of the lump, because he had seen too many bad lumps. He seemed like such an asshole right then, but he must have been scared.

I cried through the whole movie, *The Bridges of Madison County*, not because I was sad, but because I was so worried about the lumps I had found in the shower, and I couldn't believe that Tyler seemed like he didn't even care. It was a kind of cathartic and safe place to sob—everyone walked out of that movie sniffling. When I mentioned the lumps again after the movie, he had that same tone of voice. He was so dismissive that I almost believed I was a hypochondriac.

Until I told my gynecologist. The remaining lump (the other two went away after my period) was buried so deep in the right corner of my right breast near my armpit that she couldn't feel it at first. I had to guide her hand all the way into my breast.

"Geralyn. It's probably nothing because you are so young. But I never play games with lumps. You need a sonogram."

It was especially cruel timing. I mean, not that there's ever any good time to get breast cancer, but I was there to tell my gynecologist that I was ready to get pregnant. Instead of leaving her office with a prescription for prenatal vitamins, I left with a prescription for a sonogram of the lump. A sonogram turned into a mammogram, which then became a biopsy. No one with white coats in those white rooms was treating me like a hypochondriac. I wished I were a hypochondriac. I wished that my husband was right. I thought about all the petty gloats I had had whenever I was right in arguments. But there was no gloating now, just terror, with Dr. B and Tyler and the results we have just heard about my biopsy.

The first thing that I need to do is tell my little brother, Howard, who is in the waiting room. He is not really little, he's twenty-three, but he was like my baby growing up. I want to lie and protect him from this bad news.

Howard hugs me and tells me that everything will be okay. Howard will later offer to drop out of law school to take care of me. He offers to take night courses so that he can take me to every chemo. I will cry when I hear his kindness, but my parents and I convince him that his life has to go on even if mine is screeching to a halt. Howard walks with me and Tyler the four blocks back to our apartment on 96th Street between Park and Madison. I see a chalkboard outside our favorite neighborhood bistro that says "Today's Specials." As I pass that sign, I think of how easy those decisions had been—whether to have soup or salad—and how I stumbled over them. I remember how angry I was at myself because I had forgotten to drop off Tyler's shirts at the dry cleaners that morning.

When we get back to our apartment, Tyler cries until he starts honking his nose when he blows it.

"Geralyn, please, please don't leave me. I'm so scared we're going to break up. People who get cancer, they leave their marriages."

What? His comment totally floors me. I am the one who should be worried about being left. I am the damaged goods. The nurse at my biopsy already implied how "lucky" I am that I am married (as if I can't even flirt now).

That night, I decide to make a list of everyone I need to call to say that I have cancer. I don't want anyone to hear it secondhand. Like secondhand smoke, or clothing, it's not as good as the original and I realize that there is etiquette even in cancer. I get through the first call to my parents in Philadelphia. My dad keeps saying, "You have cancer? Really?" Then they start to wail. And, as if on cue, the fire alarm goes off. They must have been cooking dinner when I called and now it is burning. My mom says the house is crying. They still live in the same house in Philadelphia where I lived since I was two years old. I make my other brother, Paul, drive out to their house to make sure they are okay. He's a lawyer in Philly. What am I thinking? When I tell Paul, *he* sounds out of his mind. How could I think that he could take care of anyone? Who is taking care of him?

I keep calling everyone on my list. I even put my old boyfriend, Brian, on the list to call. It's strange, but I want him to know. I am so scared to call Jen. Her mom just had breast cancer. How can she deal with more breast cancer? My friends are outraged that the doctors in the room were the ones crying. Isn't that supposed to be my role? Weren't they supposed to comfort me and be the strong ones? But there was something that I liked about these two men in their white coats of authority suddenly feeling as helpless as I do.

The next morning, at 8:45 on the last Friday in July, instead of heading off to my job as an assistant story editor at ABC News 20/20 I am sitting in the Park Avenue office of a famous breast surgeon. I had a good excuse not to be at work that morning, although I lied to my bosses and told them I had a sore throat. I have been waiting for over half an hour to see her, and I know instead of feeling annoyed by the wait I should feel grateful. She squeezed me into her packed schedule because Tyler called her in a panic when we found out the news last night. Tyler worked for her on the breast service and told me that all of her women patients adore her because she is so tough. He said they loved her warrior mode because they thought she would be that aggressive with the cancer.

Her office is slightly below street level, and there are grates on the windows and not much light. I see the people hurrying by. Children being tugged to camp by their parents, people running to work. It feels right that I am only watching them go about their normal lives now, because nothing about my life will be normal again. Her desk is beautiful steel and glass, and it is gleaming. I notice the reflection of more glass, and pictures of a child. I don't think I will ever be able to have one now.

The order in her office is offering me a sort of refuge from this chaos. Her impressive diplomas are speaking to me from their gold frames. They are telling me that they will help me, they will cure me. I think about my own diplomas. About how hard I worked my entire life, studying, trying to get A's, just to get those diplomas to put on my resumé, to get that job. And now sitting in this chair, nothing seems to matter anymore. The diploma, the job, the marriage, the future, all feel like they are about to vaporize with that one word: cancer.

Now I am getting angry. There is nothing I can do to change the results. This is not about studying, working hard, getting the right answer, charming the right person, or nailing the interview. I spent so much of my life worrying. I thought of myself as a Chicken Little of sorts. Yes, the sky is always falling down, but not really—until now. I am a chronic worrier. A catastrophizer, actually. If that word existed, it is because someone knows me. I fret and agonize about everything and nothing at all. Maybe my worrying is a lame way of controlling my world; maybe a lifetime of silly worrying could somehow have prepared me for a real catastrophe?

When the surgeon enters the room she barely looks at me. It is my pathology report that matters here. I have been reduced to a cell type. A bad one. No small talk about what I do or how she knows Tyler. God, I would do anything for chitchat, please, please, let's at least talk about the weather? She is fishing for my mammogram. She holds a film up to the light and looks distressed. Almost as if I had snuck into a parking spot she had been eyeing or caused her to break a perfectly manicured nail. Annoyed, that is the emotion I sense. She picks up my file and that is when she finally looks at me.

"Oh my god, do you have bad luck! You are only twenty-seven? This is unbelievable."

I start to cry. No, sob. A doctor has just told me that I have bad luck? She seems bothered.

"Please pull yourself together," she is pleading now. "We have a lot to talk about."

All I can think about is that I want my mommy. She is in the waiting room. She took the train up first thing this morning from Philadelphia to be with me at this appointment; she will come with me to every doctor's appointment. I think that she insists on being here now because she was so busy working full-time with three kids when I was little.

"You need to have a double mastectomy. Meet me in the examining room."

She tries telling me a joke in the examining room. Something lame like, "Pink is your color," when she sees me in the examining gown. It is too late for any laughing now.

I want to tell her who I was yesterday, before I knew I had cancer. I want to compare notes on the last great sushi restaurant we ate at or the last pair of fabulous black strappy high heels we bought. Anything to show we still have something in common. I want her to understand that this is not my fault.

I cry so hard that she decides to have a social worker call my house later that day to check up on me, because clearly this is not part of her job—she is just the doctor. I can't stop crying. It's the first time I have cried since hearing the news. And I am crying because I think she has told me that I am incurable. That I am a walking death sentence. That she has only read about cases like mine in her medical school textbooks. I never heard of a doctor telling a patient she had bad luck. My first doctor cried, my second doctor told me I had bad luck. I am screwed.

I kind of felt like I was cheating on my boyfriend when Dr. B insisted that I get a second opinion. Would I like the other doctor more? Were there any rules about pissing off the first doctor with what the second doctor said? Dr. B recommended a lumpectomy, but this second doctor wants me to have a double mastectomy. She sees how much this news panics me and she offers to give me the phone number of a woman in the Hamptons who recently had a double mastectomy. All I can think about is, "What kind of bathing suit is she wearing now?" Since the second doctor has such a different opinion from the first, I decide I need a third-opinion doctor.

My doctor husband still can't stop crying. He must think I am going to die. He must be thinking about the twenty-eight-year-old woman he took care of on his breast rotation who was dying. He watched her die of breast cancer. I am about to turn twenty-eight in a few weeks. He is spending all his time in the medical library, pulling every study on breast cancer, reading his medical textbooks every night. He won the golden scalpel award in med school, but nothing could prepare him for this. He has taken a few days off to come with me to my doctor appointments, but then he needs to go back to the hospital, to his patients. But being in a hospital when your wife has cancer is not so easy. He is sent home from the hospital his first day back because his hands cannot stop shaking while he was scrubbing in for surgery.

I continue to see doctors. Nine strangers feel me up. Since we have already gone to second base, there are things about me that I want them to know: I wear black almost every day. I am a Leo. I wear sunglasses even on cloudy days. I am an incurable slob. "Desperado" was my favorite song even before this happened to me.

But they all keep looking at me in the same way. No eye contact. I make jokes, I wear beautiful suits and lots of perfume and lipstick to catch their attention. I am being too obvious. Tyler even tells me on the way to one consult that I look like a prostitute. I know he is terrified to see the way the other doctors are looking at me. I know he is so sweet to his patients, but maybe even he has looked at a patient this way—just right through them. I am just trying to get their attention. I want them to look at *me* and realize I am not the cancer. I am not the malignancy.

But something has happened: *I* don't exist anymore.

I've become a lab report. I want to remember a time when I could sit in the room and the doctors didn't look through me as if I had already died. I want them to know that I got to dance with Elvis Costello on stage during a concert, that I say "I'm sorry" too much, that I always change my mind, so how can I make this decision?

It keeps getting worse. I need to pick chemotherapy drugs, because my tumor was over one centimeter. I even need to choose how I will get them—high-dose IV, or pills and IV. I am offered clinical trials. I am not qualified to be making these decisions. The stakes are so high that I can't make the wrong choice.

I keep going to see famous doctors at famous hospitals: these are the Chanel, Gucci, and Prada of cancer. The doctors at one designer hospital are so famous that I am kept waiting for five hours in the waiting room. The doctors try to convince me that I need to do a clinical trial—that they created, of course—for my chemo. I can get more powerful drugs with a clinical trial, but when I ask them to walk me through the pros and cons, they seem annoyed. There are some pretty large cons: possible heart failure and early menopause. The pro: less than half a percent greater chance of a cure.

"Why should I do this clinical trial?"

"To benefit womankind," one of them says, as if I should be in a heroic mood, because I might die anyway?

"My daughter will benefit womankind *after* she survives this disease," my mother snaps back.

What one of the doctors tells me next stuns me: "It's very

strange, but all of my patients diagnosed with breast cancer get very good luck. Amazing things will happen to you."

I never knew that so many doctors actually believed in "luck," and that there is no consensus about whether I have bad luck or good luck and what I should do. I thought this was all about facts.

Whether I have good luck or bad luck, meeting so many doctors makes me realize that I am sick of being looked through and I need to devise a plan. They responded when I challenged them. They were angry, almost amused that my mother questioned their authority—that I asked them about the pros and cons. I decide that I am at a huge disadvantage. I can't speak about my cancer cell types (yes, there is more than one type of cancer cell) and I don't know the medical literature. I realize that I need to start showing these doctors who is really in control of her destiny.

My friend Jen's mom, Jane, is a breast cancer survivor and she gave me two books on breast cancer when I was first diagnosed, with an inscription: *Knowledge is power!* I am unable to even open them. Jane is a ballbuster attorney, and she arranges my next consult with her own doctor and comes with me. She asks a lot of questions about my tumor and my prognosis. She is blunt and funny and suddenly we are all laughing. She is working the doctor's office like she must work the courtroom, with some objections, but always polite. I am watching. I take notes. She gets me to ask for a copy of my pathology report. I see very scary words like *extensive intraductal carcinoma* and *poorly differentiated*—words that I would not want on my report card, and that are now describing me. Technical words about "clean" margins and estrogen receptor status being "negative." I need to figure it all out.

Jane inspires me to keep seeing doctors and to keep asking tough questions, because they are all telling me that it is my decision. My decision? I didn't go to med school. I didn't complete a surgical residency. This is ridiculous.

My training to be a reporter at the Columbia School of Journalism, and all the research I have done on stories at my new job at 20/20 didn't even come close to this story. My life is riding on this story.

I start taking notes in a reporter's notebook like the ones I use at my job at ABC News. My file becomes my secret weapon. I spend hours in the Mount Sinai medical library. I pull every article I can about breast cancer and young women. I memorize the words in my pathology report: *lobular* (sounds like a type of pasta), *intraductal* (nice to meet you cancer).

But it is still so confusing deciding whether to have a mastectomy or a lumpectomy. All the male doctors are telling me that I can have a lumpectomy, which means I can keep my breast. Basically, they would only remove a small section of tissue around where my tumor was to make sure there are "clean margins," meaning no more cancer cells. But I would then need radiation afterwards to zap any remaining cancer cells left. As part of the lumpectomy pitch, there are code words about leaving me "unchanged." They are quoting a long-term study out of Italy that sounds like a brand of Italian designer shoes. The study found that women lived just as long whether they had a mastectomy or lumpectomy. But when I pull the study on Medline, I discover that I don't even qualify for it because my tumor had an "extensive intraductal component." When I tell this to a doctor his eyebrows go up and I can tell it is working.

The women doctors have boobs and are so over it. They are telling me mastectomy. Cut it off and get it out of there. I sense a booby bias: The men think it will be too hard for me to lose my breast. In fact, there is a whole movement in the cancer world called "breast conservation." Jane says it sounds like a forest protection program.

At the end of each of my medical consults, every doctor tells me that it is my choice. It isn't fair. I want this decision made for me. They need to understand that I am an ambivalent person, that just last week I couldn't decide whether to serve hot food or cold food at my friend's bridal shower. And they are the doctors, they are supposed to know what to do. I try to bypass the system: I close the door and ask them in a lowered voice, "What would you tell your daughter to do? What would you tell your wife to do?" They still dodge.

Tyler tells me he has made up his mind after listening to all of his doctor colleagues, but that he didn't want to tell me what he thinks I should do until he hears what I want. He doesn't want to influence me.

I go back to Dr. B, the first doctor, who cried, because I like his vulnerability. He looks me in the eyes. I exist. I want to see him when I wake up after surgery.

I choose a lumpectomy like he recommended. I save everything—I even have my kindergarten report card and all my baby teeth, every love letter I ever received. I know that I can't give away my breast.

But the day before my lumpectomy, I am stumbling.

My best friend, Robin, calls me from France. She had a family trip planned before I was diagnosed and didn't want to go. I made her go.

"Rob, what should I do?" I am sobbing into the overseas phone line. "No one will tell me what to do."

"Ger, you'll know what to do. You always do."

Robin's faith in me shows me that I can make a choice and finally trust it.

The most awful thing about my ultimate decision is that it still doesn't guarantee I would live. I could cut off my breast and still die. That feels like it is the cruelest part after such a big sacrifice.

I call Dr. B. I am scared he will think that I am challenging his authority. I am scared that I will get him into trouble, because we were already on the books for lumpectomy surgery tomorrow, and this seems more serious than canceling a haircut appointment. "Dr. B, I think I should have a mastectomy instead."

I pull out my medical file and list the reasons for my decision. He is silent. And then, "Geralyn, you've convinced me. You've made the harder, smarter decision."

When I call Tyler to explain that I have cancelled my lumpectomy surgery and decided to have the mastectomy, he tells me that he's been hoping for that all along. He just didn't want to sway me. My husband must love me, I realize when I hang up the phone. But what is "me," and can he really deal with what is ahead?

Even though I have just planned my cancer treatments, I need to believe that I have a future, too. That Tyler and I have a future. I decide to see one more doctor that no one referred me to. I need to see a fertility specialist. I might die, but I need to believe I might live.

During all my consults, the cancer doctors wanted no role in my baby plan, and they tried to convince me that the song I should be listening to is "Stayin' Alive," not "She's Having a Baby." So I find a fertility specialist on my own. When I go on the Internet, the information is bleak. I make eleven calls explaining my situation, and only one doctor calls me back. I can barely hear him when I return his call on a pay phone. I strain to hear the words, "Very serious."

When I arrive at his Park Avenue fertility office, the first thing I see—well, anyone would notice—is a wall full of babies. Smiling babies, beautiful babies, perfect babies. Babies. I know it is supposed to be hopeful, but it feels like a cruel taunt.

"Na-na-na-na-na—I had a baby and you can't. Because you have cancer."

The fertility doctor puts a probe inside my vagina to check out my eggs. I am embarrassed because I have been so busy planning my surgery and chemo strategies that I forgot to shave my legs. He's a really young-looking, Doogie Howser type of doctor, and when I see his diploma on the wall I realize that we graduated from the University of Pennsylvania the same year. Maybe he will like me better knowing that my eggs were educated at the same place he went to school? Maybe he will try harder for my eggs?

After I wipe the pelvic probe goop off my unshaven legs, I hear the news I have been dreading. I read some articles about banking eggs—basically, it's like putting your eggs in a safety deposit box before chemotherapy. That way, the poison won't pollute the eggs, and in case I go into early menopause from the chemo, I'll still have eggs put away on ice. The only problem is that in order to get the eggs to bank, they need to hyper-stimulate me with hormones, and the hormones could kick my cancer into high gear.

"Ethically, no one would give you hormones now, Geralyn. I'm sorry. I could go in and grab one egg just before you menstruate, before you start your chemo, but you need to have surgery to get that one egg and the chance of that one egg surviving isn't worth it. Usually we need to work with at least four eggs just to get one that takes."

I am heartbroken that I can't bank my eggs. What would I do for a safety deposit box now?

I come up with a Plan B: I will just hit pause and get treated for my cancer and then get pregnant. But it's not that easy. When I announce my brilliant plan to my fertility doctor there is silence. It is very likely, he tells me, that I will go into early menopause from the chemo. Even worse, my cancer might return after my treatment. That would mean more chemo, and then I would definitely go into menopause if I hadn't already.

I try to start planning for every variation of my future, any future. I am desperate for a pair of headlights to show me I do have a future, even a glimmer of it.

I need to know it is there.

3

Headlights

I cannot stop thinking about the fact that I only have one week left with my breast.

And I cannot lift my head off the table at my favorite French bistro because it is hitting me that I might die. Tyler and my mom brought me here to cheer me up right after we left my bone scan appointment at the radiology suite to see if my cancer has spread to other parts of my body.

"Geralyn, honey, please lift your head up. Come on."

My arms are covering my head and my cheek is flat against the soft white linen tablecloth. I think it's the white linen tablecloth that is triggering my terror: It is reminding me of the white hallways of the hospital that I just left.

"Please, please, please lift your head up. Everything is going to be okay."

My mom sounds so desperate as she asks my favorite waitress to bring me a glass of champagne. I know my mom and Tyler are trying to get my mind off the cancer but it isn't working. They have both been with me at all these horrible consults and we all need a change of scenery. It is backfiring. At first they were laughing at me when I put my head down, but now that it's been over twenty minutes with my head down they have stopped laughing. They are panicking and don't know what to do.

I am panicking, too. It is a strange countdown, knowing that a week from now I will be in the hospital having my breast cut off of me. The panic hits me at inconvenient moments like this one when I realize that I'm a cancer patient now.

I definitely do not belong in the world of soup of the day, what should I wear today, news of the day. When the waitress comes back with my champagne I start to sob, and my back is moving up and down, and my head is still down on the table. I hear muffled voices, the waitresses are starting to whisper about the meltdown at table six, and the other chic patrons must be beginning to notice that I will not lift up my head because my mom and Tyler are pleading with me, begging me.

"Geralyn, it's not so bad. It seems like the cancer hasn't spread—we should be relieved."

I'm glad I took philosophy courses in college because I realize that I must be having an existential crisis. I am not part of this world anymore. I always cared what people thought of me and in the past I would have been too self-conscious to lose it in this tiny tony place, but in the past I didn't have cancer. I should smell the chocolate soufflé in the air and the warm summer breeze wafting through the large open doors, but all I can smell is the scary smell of the radiology suite. Instead of quiche I smell the alcohol I was swabbed with before the nurse put the rubber band on my arm to make my vein jump for the shot that injected the contrast dye. Instead of the baguettes the waitress has just put down on the table, I still smell the stench of disappointment in the air.

All I want to do is keep my head on the table and have a one-woman pity party because that visit to the radiology suite has kept me in that world of dying. I can't switch the channel in my mind to be here in the restaurant. I am still encapsulated in some huge Star Wars machine. I am reliving that hour in the bone scan.

When the technician asked me if I was claustrophobic right before he put me into the huge machine, it made me think about all the things that I'm really scared of now that I have cancer. He dimmed the lights and I considered telling him that I am actually scared of the dark or pretending I'm a claustrophobic so I could get out of this thing. Because I am terrified I can't handle more bad news. I'm scared of dying before I turn thirty.

The lab technician looked so serious that he was making me even more scared. Why couldn't he just smile—would it kill him?

When the machine started to rumble I was embarrassed to remember the things that used to scare me:

Cockroaches.

Wearing no makeup and running into an old boyfriend who broke my heart.

Algebra.

Having to ride from the lobby up to the tenth floor alone with Barbara Walters at work—how do I make conversation for ten straight floors?

Having to tell my doorman that I forgot my key to my apartment again and could I borrow the secret key just one more time?

The dark (I always sleep with a nightlight on).

Now I am just scared that my cancer has spread.

I am scared they will tell me they can't cure me and that I only have months to live.

I am scared they will discover that the pain in my neck is actually a huge tumor and not a pulled muscle from trying to look cool at the gym.

I am scared that people at work are just being nice because they think I might die.

I am scared my husband secretly thinks he married damaged goods.

I am scared not enough people will come to my funeral. I am scared that I did not amount to enough. I am scared that I will not have an obituary. Scared that my student loans will not even be paid off when I die (I checked the fine print and felt a little better knowing that they can't make you pay if you've died). I am scared that my younger brother Howard will not be able to handle his big sister dying on him. I'm his big sister and I'm supposed to protect him. I am scared I have let so many people down by getting cancer. It is so strange to have cancer at twenty-seven. I'm not a kid with cancer—that is super tragic. But I am still young enough that it is quasi-kid tragic. I feel like such a baby having my parents there with me at my doctor appointments. But I need my mommy and daddy now. I was never scared of monsters when I was little. I am so scared of cancer now.

I am scared to go to sleep because I think I won't wake up. I will just close my eyes and I won't even know that I died. Is that how people die? Will I know that I died? I am scared on rainy and cold nights that I will be lonely when I die, that I will miss everyone. I am scared I won't be missed.

I am scared that my cancer is incurable. That it is aggressive—I mean, how could I ever have a passive cancer? No way. Just ask my Dad. I am scared sometimes when it is quiet that the cancer is starting to grow again. That it is swishing around my body as my heart is beating.

I am scared that I will never be the same.

That is why now I can't just sit in a restaurant and pretend I am part of the normal world. Why should I even eat if I am dying anyway? I hear silverware rattling and I know that Tyler and my mom are starting to eat their lunch. I lift my head up a little and peek through my arm and I see the worry in Tyler's and my mom's eyes, but I also see they were optimistic enough to order me my favorite meal: a smoked salmon platter. They are picking at their food and look as panicked as I feel. I can't do this to them. I need to be brave for them. I need to lift up my head.

"I'm sorry," I start to sob again. I sound so muffled through my arms. "Let me take an Ativan and see if I can calm down. I promise I'll try to eat in a few minutes."

I have been trying to learn how to manage my anxiety and right now in this restaurant is the perfect test. I am trying to remind myself about my newfound secret weapons: Ativan, Affirmations, and Amazons . . .

Ativan: All my boob doctors have been telling me that I need a head doctor because clearly they are two different specialties. Whenever I ask, "Am I going to die?" or "Why did this happen to me?" or whenever I cry, they tell me, "You need to see a psychiatrist."

Tyler found me my cancer therapist. She had written a book about treating cancer patients and their families that was displayed in the Mount Sinai medical library. She lets me say anything I need to, like, "I'm scared I'm going to die," and "Why did this happen to me?" It doesn't freak her out at all or make her think that I am crazy. But she, too, told me, "You need to see a psychiatrist." But not because she was worried that I was going crazy. She wanted me to get a prescription for anti-anxiety medication: Ativan. Whoever invented Ativan must have been a very worried person because it really does take the edge off nicely.

Affirmations: I also found a hypnotherapist to teach me how to say affirmations to calm myself down because I am so scared I will faint when I get needles. I have such a low pain threshold and I can't stand blood. I faint even seeing blood donation signs. The hypnotherapist tells me to think of myself as like the sky and then nothing can stick to me. The sky is so open and vast and stays unchanged no matter what; it is always the sky. A storm can roll through it, an airplane can roar through, and it is always the sky.

"I am like the sky and nothing can stick to me," is what I say before every needle now, and it is working.

She tells me to write a note that my doctor can read to me when he is putting me under anesthesia before my mastectomy surgery. She asks me what I am scared of and then she puts a spin on it. I tell her that I am scared of scalpels. She tells me the scalpel is my friend. I tell her I am scared that my doctors will make a mistake on me. She tells me that I am in a room full of experts. I tell her that I am scared my cancer will come back. She tells me that I

am cured. I tell her that I am scared that I will regret the mastectomy after my breast has been cut off. She tells me that I am proud
of the decision I made. I tell her that I am so embarrassed at how
wimpy I am. I feel like a coward. Everyone tells me that I am brave
but I am filled with terror and self-doubt. She tells me the story of
how she finally mastered her fear by doing a fire walk over coals.
She was terrified. She was doing it with a group of five women as
part of a training seminar. Four of them talked nonstop about how
scared they were to do the fire walk. How they thought they might
get burned. How they might get halfway through and not be able
to finish. The fifth woman never said she was scared. She was the
one who got third degree burns halfway over the hot coals. The
other four made it without a blister. My hypnotherapist is telling
me that being scared is brave.

"It is so courageous to live by your heart. You need to honor
your fear." She explains to me the root of the word *courage* is *coeur*
or heart. That following your heart is a form of real courage because it is so hard to listen to your heart. I always thought that following my heart was just the easy way out. The idea that it is
actually an act of courage, that somehow my fear is strength, makes
me feel less weak.

But since I have been following my heart so much in these past
few weeks, it is beating wildly and I can't tame it. The Ativan
helps. And when my medication or affirmations fail, I have still
found the best therapy of all. Actually, she found me.

When I first heard her voice on my answering machine, it was
the only time I had heard my future since my diagnosis. Just from
her voice, I know that she must be powerful and bold and the stuff
of myths. She is an Amazon.

"Geralyn, my name is Rena. You don't know me. I'm your friend

Jon's aunt and I had breast cancer years and years ago." Her voice becomes my lifeline. She tells me about her mastectomy, her chemo, but what she is really telling me is how alive she is all these years later. She signs everything "In Celebration!" She tells me to wear my best jewelry to the hospital. I tried a support group right after I was diagnosed but it didn't work for me: Everyone was comparing tumor size and estrogen receptor status, and I found myself wanting to solve everyone's problems in the room except for mine. Rena is different. She wants to tell me everything that helped her and to be my guide. She is convincing me I will have a future. How is she so brave for me? I go onto the Internet and look up Amazons. Women warriors who sliced off their breasts so that they could pull their arrows back further. They were serious. Bad-ass. I channel the voice of Rena and I hear the voice of a warrior. Of a woman who did anything to survive. I know I will cut off my breast, too. But am I Amazon material?

The Ativan and the champagne have finally settled in as a nice buzz (oops, I remember the warning said not to drink alcohol while taking Ativan, but it is already too late). Will I ever be an Amazon? I am made of the stuff of myths?

Maybe just lifting up my head is the first step. A small step to re-enter the world I am sure that I have already left. If life is short, I need a sip of champagne and a bite of chocolate soufflé. And, maybe one more Ativan, too? I love those and I am so glad I finally did see a psychiatrist. As I lift up my head I feel dizzy and see some black spots from my head being down so long. I can see my mom's and Tyler's smiles as I squint in the bright sunlight. I order a cappuccino to counter the Ativan/champagne buzz, and when I hear the milk steaming it sounds like the bone scan sounded when it stopped whirring. I realize that the things that used to scare me feel so softball compared to an hour in a bone scan machine.

Bring it on.

My eyes are swollen and my nose is running so I grab the napkin on my lap. My mascara is all over the white tablecloth and my lipstick has left a thick red smear across the table, too. I'm not embarrassed. I don't care anymore. My mom and Tyler and the waitresses and the customers think that I am unraveling.

But I know that it is just my courage starting to show.

4

I Need to Get It Off My Chest

It is my twenty-eighth birthday and I am actually supposed to be having a mastectomy today, but when Dr. B realized it was my birthday he refused. He didn't want me to think about this on every subsequent birthday. But I am so not convinced there will be that many more to celebrate. I just want to hit thirty.

More important than celebrating my birthday, I need to some-how mark the last day of wearing my girly costume: Today is my last day with both my breasts, and just yesterday they told me that I definitely have to do six months of chemo. So my long black hair is about to disappear, too. How do I mark this day? I decide I should go outside and get street-harassed for one last time.

I need a day to *not* talk about cancer. I need a break, because I have been telling everyone. It has only been two weeks since my breast cancer diagnosis and I'm still adjusting to what my new life as a cancer patient will be. It is so strange that I look and feel exactly the same—but everything is different.

My parents and my brother Paul have come in from Philly to help me celebrate my birthday with Howard and Tyler and to be with me for my surgery tomorrow. I can't tell them about my plan because I'm too embarrassed to admit it, but I am so incredibly desperate for some attention before it all goes away.

I always hated it when men would catcall or leer and I always shouted back something lewd at them or gave them the finger, but now I want it so bad.

I've got to leave my nine-hundred-square-foot, one-bedroom apartment because it is not big enough to handle all the well wishes mingled with grief. Every minute the phone is ringing with high-drama "Happy Birthdays," or the I-never-told-you-how-much-I-loved-you-but-now-that-you-have-cancer-I-want-to-show-you flowers are arriving.

I need to clear my mind of cancer for just one afternoon. I want to have some fun and not talk about my tumor size or chemo regimen. I've been talking nonstop about cancer now for over two weeks, inappropriately telling strangers that I have cancer. I even tell the male stripper at a bachelorette party. I make it come up in conversation because I've been reading articles that suggest that breast cancer happens because women repress things and hold them close to their chests. I think it's bullshit, but I need to cover all my bases—but did I have to tell the poor deli guy? "Sorry, I won't have my regular coffee because I was just diagnosed with cancer and a macrobiotic nutritionist told me that caffeine makes tumors grow." (My parents have insisted that I start eating health food since my diagnosis.) My deli guy sort of looked at me like it was too much information, and it was.

But I couldn't tell my Grandma Ruth that I have cancer. It would have been too sad for her and, because she is losing her mind, I was scared that I'd tell her and then she'd forget and then I'd need to tell her again, and how many times could she stand to hear that her granddaughter has cancer?

I had seventeen bridesmaids at my wedding and four matrons of honor, so there were a lot of people I had to call. But should I have told my flower girl, Alissa? She is only seven and worships me and I can't die on her. The telling had gotten a little easier, sort of like when I waited tables in college and I rattled off the daily specials. I wanted all my family and friends to hear it directly from me, to have front-row seats to what was unfolding, rather than hear it from someone else and think that they were not close enough to my heart.

When I told Robin, she started to make almost animal noises and dropped the phone. After she picked it up, she couldn't stop sobbing,

"No, no, no. I love you."

She has always been more emotional than I am, and I've counted on her my entire life to be the part of me I could not be. We have been best friends since we were three, and our parents still live across the street from each other in Philadelphia. Robin is my alter ego. She cried when they separated us in first grade because we were too cliquey. I wanted to cry, too, but I am more distant from my feelings. Robin is in charge of calling our two other best friends, Jane and Diane, because my call with Robin shows me that I can't handle the calls with Jane and Diane, especially since

Diane is on vacation in Africa and we don't want her to get on a plane and rush home.

The one person I was most scared to tell was my boss, Meredith. I was dreading it because she is a goddess and thoroughly intimidating. Meredith is so perfect, and this news was so messy. I had been trying to win her over with the best story ideas and working late, and it was hard to tell if I was impressing her because because she was just so composed.

My lawyer brothers, Paul and Howard, had researched the law for me and told me it would be illegal for ABC to fire me. I wasn't worried about that, I was just worried that they would think so much less of me and write off my future there.

I had finally landed my dream job at *20/20*, and I had been there less than a year. I was so star struck finally getting hired at *20/20* because I got to watch Barbara Walters walk back and forth in front of my cubicle on her way to the bathroom. I rode in the elevator with Hugh Downs. Now it felt like all that, too, was going to be taken away. Even if my breast and hair were gone, at least I thought I would still have my brain. But now I wasn't so sure. Television is the kind of career where someone might see your cancer as a career opportunity. *Damaged goods*, was all I was thinking. They'd consider me some sort of medical oddity. I really wanted to make a good impression and now I needed to tell them I had cancer?

Maybe I could just keep it a secret. Could I pull that off? Maybe they would just think I got a boob job after my reconstructive surgery and I could wear a wig and maybe no one would notice.

I practiced my speech, trying to sound professional and in control, but when Meredith picked up the phone I just blurted. I was always scared anyway of being inarticulate around Meredith because she is so smart.

There was silence and then: "Geralyn, I had breast cancer when I was younger, in my thirties."

What? I never knew!

She is so perfect. She is so beautiful. She has lived. "Meredith, please don't tell anyone. I'm so embarrassed. I don't want anyone else to know."

"Geralyn. You'll need all of our support. I'll tell everyone for you. Don't worry about that. I don't want you to be burdened telling everyone."

She didn't want me to have to deal with everyone's reactions. She told the whole staff. She organized a staff present, and a gigantic get-well card signed by every single person who worked at *20/20*. Meredith even told Barbara Walters. Barbara sent me a hand-written note: *Geralyn, you are so beautiful and smart and we are all waiting for your return.*

Even though Meredith took care of the telling, I had to go to the office one more time the Sunday after my diagnosis because I needed to clean up my desk and get my work in order. I was the first person to hold the position of assistant story editor, so no one was really sure of what I did. I find story ideas for *20/20* segments. I read local papers from all over the country and the news wires and strange publications to find interesting, untold stories. And I have found some pretty amazing ones: Amish runaways, kids who want to meet their sperm donor dads, a woman who had twenty-seven plastic surgeries to make herself look like a Barbie doll.

I typed up my job description and made a list of all the stories I was currently working on and what was ready to be assigned to a producer. It felt so responsible of me to be doing this, but it was also a relief to take my mind off cancer cell types for a few hours, and to be back where I could actually use my brain and where no one needed to feel me up *again.*

I had not seen or spoken to anyone since Meredith ran interference for me. I did not expect to see anyone in the office on a Sunday, but there he was. The big Kahuna, my boss's boss, the executive producer, Victor, in his tennis outfit. I wanted to put my head down and pray that he wouldn't notice me, but in a strange way I needed to tell him that he could count on me, and that just because I had cancer I was not going away.

"Victor. Hi. I'm just getting some of my things together before I have my surgery . . ."

I could see that I was totally freaking Victor out, and to make matters worse, I grabbed his hand! I never held my boss's hand! What is wrong with me?

"I'm going to be fine. I scheduled my chemo for Fridays so I can rest over the weekend and be back at work on Mondays."

Victor looked concerned but uncomfortable and just kept nodding. I knew that I was coming on so strong to convince us both that I would live and that he could count on me to do my job. I had been trying to impress Victor by getting the best stories for *20/20,* but now I needed to convince him that I would live. I remembered how hard I had tried to get hired, how I used to jump when I heard his booming voice on the other end of the phone, and I couldn't believe we had just held hands. Wow, this getting-it-off-my-chest stuff was pretty powerful! That encounter with Victor showed me that I clearly couldn't handle telling, and that Meredith was a much more graceful and thorough publicist.

Since my diagnosis I had been looking for another young woman who had been through this. I had only heard of my mom's friends, grandmothers. Had angels planned for Meredith to be my boss? Could this be real? This was crazy! And it was about to get even crazier.

I was about to become completely convinced of angels—on my twenty-eighth birthday, the day before my mastectomy.

I painstakingly pick out my outfit for my last hurrah, my pre-mastectomy I-need-some-attention-I-need-it-so-badly strut. I'm wearing my favorite faded jeans that make my butt look awesome. And a bodysuit that is very tight and accentuates my breasts—I'm not wearing a bra . . . I never do because my breasts are small and firm enough.

It's ninety-five degrees and the city is deserted. Everyone must be away at the beach, but I am stuck here waiting for my surgery to-morrow. I put my hand up to hail a taxi and two start to race to-wards me. Maybe it's because there are so few fares today in this scorching heat, or maybe my outfit is working? Is this why the taxis are lurching towards me? The one farther away darts in front of the other taxi and does a sharp turn towards me, nearly causing a rear-end collision. After some heavy screaming and door-slamming and *fuck-yous!* I reluctantly enter the winner, and it's about to become clear exactly why he has won.

I'm just relieved to slide into some air conditioning, because lit-tle blotches of sweat have already started to stain my bodysuit. My inadvertent wet T-shirt seems to make my cab driver quite pleased, especially because I'm not wearing a bra. This is shaping up to be quite the last hurrah for my breasts.

"Hello, LADY!" He is screaming at me over some blaring dance music that sounds like the club mixed version of "La Bamba."

Oh, no . . . I'm noticing that he has a small disco ball hanging in his rearview mirror. It is reminding me of the disco ball over the stage where the strippers showed their boobs.

I offer back a weak "hi," pull my large black sunglasses off the top of my head and put them on, hoping to signal that I don't want any conversation on this cab ride.

"I saw you from three blocks away. Wow! I nearly crashed that other cab to meet you! My insurance goes way up if that happens!"

So now I sort of feel obligated to talk to the guy, because he risked a higher insurance rate for me.

"Oh. I just thought you were a bad driver like a lot of cabbies."

I am trying to be rude—maybe this will stop him. He must be a masochist, because he continues with even more excitement.

"No, I'm a very good driver. And dancer." He starts to hit the brakes in time with the music and I can't help but crack up.

"You like to dance, lady? Wow, I bet you look hot on the dance floor."

I think about myself on the dance floor—my breasts are shaking with the music—but then it sounds like a scratch in the record when I realize that tomorrow only one boob will be shaking on the dance floor. How will I dance? Will everyone notice that only one boob shakes and the other is reconstructed? The vision of myself as a hottie in the taxi is fading. I wanted this attention but I'm suddenly feeling very annoyed by this cab driver. It's not really his fault, but now I'm pissed that he's hitting on me. Furious, really. He doesn't know that I'm just wearing a costume because my breasts and hair are about to disappear. I know he won't leer tomorrow when I only have one boob. He won't turn his head when I lose my hair. He's compounding my grief by admiring what I've already given away in my head. He could be any man. He's leering and he wants me for things I will soon not have. I'm scared he will not want me when they are gone. Trying to be a sexy woman is making my heart so heavy now, and I feel it pounding hard.

I remember the articles I have read about repression, that holding problems close to your chest causes cancer. I've been trying to tell everyone I have cancer, but the articles say you have to go further than just confessing. The truth is hard for me. I speak in a high voice and like to sugarcoat. I don't like confrontation. It's really hard for me to get angry. I have decided the whole idea of repression causing cancer is such bullshit, but I am still covering all my bases.

So I decide I need to get it off my chest. Right here in the dancing taxi I will keep telling the truth. I will even bare my soul. This is a sign about my newfound honesty: I have nothing to lose.

"Actually, I won't be doing much dancing because tomorrow I'm having my right breast cut off because I have cancer . . ." I take a dramatic pause and peek over my sunglasses just to see if he has gotten what I just told him. "And after that all my hair will start falling out from my chemotherapy."

The cab is lurching and I think he is starting to make it dance again and I'm relieved that maybe he didn't hear what I said and I'm already feeling better because, like I will do with my cancerous breast tomorrow, I have gotten it off my chest. But he has stopped the cab, parked it actually, haphazardly, illegally even, in front of a bus stop on the southeast corner of Madison Avenue and Ninety-sixth Street.

Wow! I really shook him up, I smirk to myself. He will now definitely think twice before he leers at young girls' boobs and nearly causes an accident just to flirt. I've shown him!

And then he shows me.

He opens the door and comes to sit next to me in the back seat. Terrified, I start to move away. He's grabbing my hand and before I can pull it back he has put it to his mouth to kiss it. Gross!

"I had testicular cancer. My left ball was removed."

Okay, he must be a pervert and what a cruel way to hit on me now. As if he is reading my mind he adds credibility to his story. He mentions the cancer patients' Mecca.

"I was treated at Sloan-Kettering—three years ago. I'm fine. You will be, too."

The "La Bamba" club mix version is still blaring. And there's magic in the air because this man has turned from a frog to a prince and I'm really trying to understand what has just happened here in the back seat of this taxi on Ninety-sixth Street and Madison Avenue in front of a bus stop.

It is funny that he's the first person who can convince me that someday I will get my whole life back. I don't believe my doctors, therapist, family, or friends. I think they are just trying to reassure me, and themselves, too. But this man, he has credibility. I am looking into the next few weeks of hell and suddenly an angel with one ball has appeared to tell me that I can be whole with one boob.

He's managed to go on with one ball. He still flirts. He is still a man, maybe even more so because he is compensating for missing his other ball by being so bold. Maybe that's why he blares his music and makes his cab dance and risks having an accident just for a fare. Maybe he is out on that edge where he is really living because he almost died. Maybe it is the first time that I can see my future as a woman since my diagnosis.

He kisses my hands and he refuses my fare. I protest but I know he can't take my money. We're members of the same tribe, and any luck thrown our way we need to grab and try to believe good things can happen.

As he pulls away I smell exhaust fumes mingling with all the perfume I had put on for my last boob strut and it makes me feel slightly dizzy because this is the first time since I've been diagnosed with cancer that I can taste hope: If a one-balled man and an about-to-be-one-boobed woman can somehow end up dancing in a taxi in a city of millions and figure out this hidden truth within the span of a seven-minute cab ride, then somehow I will survive this ordeal.

5

Why I Wore Lipstick

I look at my right breast for the last time ever.

It is the morning of my mastectomy surgery. The digital clock flips to 6:33 A.M. It is still dark outside but I am standing topless in a bright fluorescent-lit cubicle about to take off my jeans and underwear before I put on the surgical gown, hair net, and paper slippers the nurse has just handed to me.

As I unzip my jeans, I do notice that strangely, there is a little mirror hanging on the wall. Who could ever be vain now? I touch the mirror to make sure this is all really happening and notice the deep bags under my eyes. I pulled an all-nighter just looking at my breast and wondering how to say good-bye. I even took a picture of it. I still can't believe that when I wake up after my surgery I will have only a blood-soaked bandage where my right breast is.

I am shivering as I tie the surgical smock. It says PROPERTY OF MT. SINAI HOSPITAL in scary black letters. I realize that I, too, strangely, am now property of the hospital. There is an old air conditioner that is making my nipple hard, and I feel a rush of sensation on my right side. What will it feel like when my breast is not there? I pile my long black hair under the hair net, hold the bangs up and push them underneath, and slide my feet into the scratchy paper slippers. I'm going through the motions, but when I look in the mirror again I start to sob.

I have Sting in my Walkman, and I'm trying to picture walking in Fields of Gold. I have written down affirmations for today that I keep reading to myself: "The scalpel is my friend." I don't care if they think I'm crazy. The cab driver has shown me I have to speak up, and I do.

There is a knock on the door and Dr. B asks if he can come in. He is in a suit and I am in scrubs. It is usually the reverse. He has come to visit me in the little cubicle and when he sees me his face drops, turning even greener than the fluorescent lights have made him look.

I know that I look horrible, and it's not just the fluorescent lighting. He is trying to rally me, but I think that the Geralyn that he knows is already gone. At least I'm pretty sure of it. I can't summon myself and I can't pretend that I'm feeling brave. I'm about to lose myself, to be cut into, and already I feel my body starting to slip away from me. I'm starting to feel each breath, wondering what it will be like to be put under anesthesia for the first time. How will I wake up from the surgery? Will I cry? Will I know as soon as I wake up that my breast is gone? Will I feel the pain first and then remember? What if I don't wake up? What if I die on the operating room table? What if they open me up and there is cancer everywhere?

"Geri. We're a team. Where's my partner? Where's the Geri that I know?"

I hate the name Geri and no one else but Dr. B calls me that. He can call me anything he wants right now because he is about to cut my boob off. How do I wrap my mind around what is happening to me? How do I willingly submit to this? How can I be complete when a piece of me is being cut away? How do I hold on to myself?

I can't believe he has come to visit me before I see him in the operating room. That is so amazing that he wanted to see me, all of me, before he has to cut off my boob. I want to be strong for him, for me, for my family, for Tyler. I think about trying to rally as Dr. B leaves the cubicle.

I remember, when I was a little girl, how I climbed to the top of my favorite tree in my backyard wearing my Mary Janes and red-and-white-dot party dress just to prove to my younger brothers that I could. I remember how I fell down from the top branch because my Mary Janes' slippery soles slid on the bark. I was proud of my skinned knee. I had earned it.

I want to earn this moment, too. I need to summon myself and own this courage that is waiting for me to grab. Right now it is anxiety and torture and dread but that courage is just begging me to own it. All I can think about is that somehow I need to be myself in this sterile room, during this surgery that has been forced on me. I need to remind everyone that I am not just another mastectomy, right side, on the OR table. I need to leave a trace that *I* was here, too, not only my boob. I can't stand the thought of anyone looking through me during such an important moment in my life, the way I felt looked through by so many doctors when I was first diagnosed.

That is when I remember my lipstick. It is almost habit—I just take it everywhere with me. I pull my lipstick out of the crinkled heap of my jeans and as carefully as I can I trace the outline of my lips. I pucker and then smooth the lipstick by rubbing my top and bottom lip together. I apply another coat. It is matte, which means it should hold up in surgery. I am glad that it is not shiny because then it might smear when they put the breathing tube down my throat. I curl my middle finger and put my knuckle in the small curve in the middle of my top lip to remove any excess and glide my pointer finger knuckle along the lower rim of my lips to make sure it looks perfect. The lipstick stains my finger and I think about the song "Lipstick on Your Collar"—maybe I will leave a little smear of lipstick in the operating room today just to let them know I was there?

I do love lipstick because no one is born with it. It is so democratic. Applying it is such a willful gesture. Lipstick is confident and demands attention. I remember all the women I watched applying lipstick in ladies' rooms. *Notice Me, I Deserve This,* they were writing on their lips with every stroke. I think about Marilyn Monroe. I am channeling her lipstick, not her boobs.

I am so glad there is a mirror because now I can see that I finally look like myself in this hair net and surgical gown. I recognize myself with my lipstick. It needs to look perfect because it will look creepy and bizarre if it is slightly smudged. That will make me look wild. I am going for defiant, and there is a difference. I want to look as deliberate as possible. It is not an accident that I am wearing lipstick. It is not left over from a wild night of partying. My lipstick will say, *Notice Me.*

I am so relieved I had my long-lasting, super-matte lipstick in my pocket. This is a high-endurance situation, more than the commercials where the model keeps eating and wiping her mouth and her lipstick is still perfect eight hours later.

When the nurse calls my name I think about how prisoners marching to their deaths somehow find one defiant gesture to mock the situation. Even as I am sedated under heavy anesthetic, and my breast is being carefully placed in the pathology lab Tupperware, maybe I can still feel attractive.

I am put on a gurney and wheeled underground through the hospital towards the operating room. After an elevator ride, I am in a bright holding area outside the operating room where they will cut off my breast. It is such a deep moment, but all I can think about is how thirsty I am, because I was not allowed to drink anything before my surgery. The night before, I had a huge lobster dinner to celebrate my birthday. Note to self: Do not eat lobster dipped in butter, rice pilaf, and crème brûlée if you're having surgery the next day. What was I thinking? Maybe it is Titanic reasoning: I am going down with violins playing. My parents made me go out to celebrate, but I drew the line at the waiter singing "Happy Birthday." There is nothing happy about this birthday. Tyler gave me a beautiful antique glass necklace for my birthday. It was such an odd gift because I can't picture wearing a necklace when I am bald and have one boob. It is a strange vote of confidence that he thinks I will still be able to wear a beautiful necklace, that his vision of who I am has not changed yet. But I'm worried about us, about what all this is doing to him. He stayed out until 4 A.M. two nights ago. He came home and smelled like beer, and when I asked him where he had been he told me that he had spent the night crying in his beer about his wife who has breast cancer to three women visiting from Australia that he just met at the bar. They all cried for me.

I see Dr. B. again, but this time he is in full surgeon mode—in all-blue scrubs with a mask—standing in the hallway just outside the operating room. Dr. Brower tells me they are setting up the OR and just need about five more minutes. Five minutes? I need an Ativan. Help. My heart is feeling so wild right now and my lipstick is making me feel even wilder.

My anesthesiologist has come to put the IV line in my arm. He is gentle but it still hurts to get the needle. I feel the smooth rush of fluids entering my vein. When he comes over to check my IV I beg him for some anti-anxiety medication. He pushes something through my IV and I feel the rush in my vein again.

How long will it take this sedative to kick in? Maybe I need to pace and say more affirmations to calm myself down? I slide off the gurney as delicately as I can and pull the IV pole along. I realize the back of my surgical gown is open and my butt is hanging out but does it matter if anyone checks it out? I am about to have my breast cut off, so there is no false modesty here.

I see the fiery red exit sign at the end of the hallway and I start shuffling towards it, dragging the IV pole, sort of like we are doing the Hustle together. The exit sign matches my bright red lipstick. It is equally defiant and it is screaming a siren song: "Bolt out the door and keep your breast. Bolt. Keep your breast. Bolt." I am trying to remember my lipstick, but all I see is the scalpel.

I know now why exit signs were invented. For dangerous situations like this: like fires, and like fleeing a building so your breast will not be cut off. My life is on fire. It is burning down around me. I don't belong here. I need to EXIT.

How did this all happen in just a matter of weeks? Why did this happen? Why me? Was it because I took birth control pills, did not go to the gym enough? Ate too many cheeseburgers? The one cigarette I smoked in ninth grade? I want to leave so badly. I have not lived my life hard enough. I have never even gotten a speeding ticket. I have lived inside the lines too much. I want to run. Would I set off an alarm if I bolted through the door? I want to just walk through the door and go back to the life I left where the "clean" I worried about was a stain on my favorite pants, not the cancer in my lymph nodes. They are removing my lymph nodes today and tomorrow I will know if my cancer has spread. That feels almost as scary as waking up without a breast.

The red letters EXIT are glowing, and showing me a safe passage back to the life I left.

But I think how crazy I would look running down Fifth Avenue in a surgical smock with my ass hanging out with a hairnet. I see strange people in New York City all the time but this would be especially creepy because I have bright red lipstick on. And where would I run to? I would be a fugitive from cancer. I might pull it off, but the IV pole would have to come, too. My IV pole is my ball and chain. I could yank it out, but I faint when I see blood, and this would be messy.

I decide not to run out the door because I am scared of what people would think of me—that, and it might make the cover of the *New York Post*. GIRL GOES WILD BEFORE MASTECTOMY SURGERY! They would write about my lipstick. I always worry about what people think, so I know I am still here. It is a good sign that I am too embarrassed to flee. It is the lipstick that saves me from leaving. I would never be able to explain why I was wearing it.

I am so scared that one of my second-opinion cancer doctors who told me that I needed to see a psychiatrist might see me now in the operating room area. Yikes. Those doctors would definitely say, "You still need to see a psychiatrist, especially because you are wearing lipstick to your mastectomy surgery." But I know that I'm not crazy. Since all the doctors told me that I am "living with risk" (risk of my cancer coming back, risk of dying) I have decided to become risqué.

I shuffle back to the stretcher, and now it is show time.

Because Tyler works in this hospital he manages to sneak my parents and brothers up through the corridors into the surgical holding area to see me one last time. What if I never wake up from the surgery? Is this our last hug? They are hugging me so hard that I am scared my IV might get pulled out. And then they are wheeling me in and it almost looks like a kitchen because there is so much stainless steel everywhere. Maybe my lipstick will shimmer its reflection in the dull surfaces.

There must be about ten people in the OR in scrubs. I realize that they only know me as twenty-eight-year-old mastectomy, right breast. But just maybe they will notice my lipstick? My lipstick feels so far away from the scalpel.

My lipstick is all I have.

I'm clinging to that thin film of beeswax or paraffin or whatever ingredients lipstick is made of. That thin layer of color, of moisture, of hope is all I have that is mine when they put the oxygen mask on my face to put me under. I am holding on so tight to that hyper-red-notice-me-now pigment that is screaming that I am out of context because I do not deserve to be in this operating room having my breast cut off.

I want my lipstick to tell everyone in this room that I think I have a future and I know I will wear lipstick again, but on my terms next time. But for now, I have my war paint. I think I am ready. I glide my tongue one last time over the smooth surface and I taste the lipstick in my mouth and it is mingling with the anesthesia cloud that has made me very sleepy and then—I am out.

If I were awake I would see Dr. B slicing away the mound of flesh that was my breast and carefully placing it in the pathology container.

If I were awake I would hear the beeping of my heart and the whirring of the breathing machine, because I am intubated.

If I were awake, I might feel a little pride that I wore such a true red shade that it now seems to perfectly match the blood on the operating room table.

If I were awake I would tell them how proud I am that I decided to cut off my breast, to hopefully save my life.

If I were awake I would tell them that I know I will still be a woman.

For anyone who does not believe this, that is why I am wearing lipstick.

In the sterility of the operating room I am laughing.

In the blood and gauze I am dancing.

Under anesthesia, with a tube forced down my throat, I am hopeful and maybe even a little sexy.

And slightly in control, just knowing that my lipstick might last.

6

Peep Show

All I can see when I try to open my eyes is the white bandage where my right breast used to be. This is the moment I've been dreading: I have woken up after my mastectomy surgery and a piece of me is gone. They are screaming at me to breathe as hard as I can in the recovery room at Mount Sinai Hospital. The recovery room is like a low-budget porn movie—lots of moaning, bad lighting, and way too much directing.

"Open your mouth—wider. Wider. Wider!"

They gave me too much anesthesia for my surgery and I feel like I'm slurping up air. I still can't breathe, even after they have rolled over the respirator and put the mask on. In between all the chaos a

sassy nurse comes over to me and screams that I need to breathe—
b-r-e-a-t-h-e harder.

"Open your mouth!" Then, just when I think she is about to
yell at me again, she starts to smile. It's the lipstick.

"Girl, what kind of lipstick are you wearing? That shit stayed
on for your six-hour surgery!"

Good thing my lipstick is not fading, because I am.

But I can see Tyler hovering above me. He is reading me the affirmations my hypnotherapist suggested: "You are cured. You are so
proud of your decision to have the mastectomy. Your body knows
exactly how to respond to the surgery."

Tyler looks as in love as he did on the night he proposed to me
in a horse-drawn carriage in Central Park. He hid two champagne
glasses and a bottle of champagne under his trench coat. After I
screamed "Yes!" and we downed the bubbly, he wanted to smash
our glasses. As we threw our glasses and the glass shattered, Tyler
grabbed me and said, "Geralyn, this moment can never be un-
done." I remember those shards of glass shining on the New York
City sidewalk under the street light. Now I feel like this surgery
has smashed me into tiny pieces that can't be glued back together.
Everything hurts so badly. Tyler looks so scared in his surgical
scrubs and so brave for me somehow. It is so strange because I
have seen him in scrubs at home many times, but never in the
hospital.

I must have blacked out because when I wake up again I know
that I am out of the recovery room—I don't hear the moaning all
around me. I am now in the hushed dim of a hospital room instead
of the bright stadium lights of the recovery room. I can hear the
sadness in the air and it feels so loud that I want to reassure everyone that I will be okay. There is a small crowd. My parents, broth-

ers, in-laws, and friends have been sitting here in the darkness waiting for me to wake up.

Robin starts to cry and my mother-in-law tells her not to cry in front of me and to leave the room. My dad is sitting and thinking hard. He looks like he is about to take a swing on the racquetball court. I strain to lift my head up and they all begin to come into focus and I can see the anticipation in the room. I try to say something but my voice is hoarse from the tube that has been down my throat during surgery.

"I feel so much performance anxiety. Please, someone else speak."

That makes everyone laugh and we begin to talk about everything except what we're all thinking about: my wound. No one will talk about it.

A young doctor comes into the room to change my dressing and everyone leaves. I try to turn my neck as far away as I can when he starts to peel away the thin white layers of gauze that I feel are wet and blotched with fresh blood. I close my eyes and remember never being able to look when I got shots when I was little. I can't look. Not yet. The doctor also unscrews the plastic drains that are sewn into my chest to catch my oozing wound fluid. He empties the fluid, screws back the drains, and checks my morphine pump. He scribbles something on my chart and quietly disappears into the bright white corridor outside my room. It would be strange to chitchat and I am way too tired to be nice or flirt.

That first night, my chest is burning and pounding because the anesthesia is wearing off. I tell Tyler how much it hurts and he tells me it's normal and to keep pushing my morphine pump for more pain meds. I keep buzzing for the nurse, but she just keeps screaming at me over the intercom that a doctor is on his way. This is definitely not *General Hospital*. Finally, four hours later, the pain resident comes to visit me. Tyler didn't want me to bother him. Tyler knows the pain resident because I am at Mount Sinai where Tyler is doing his training. His friend is confused and asks if we just had a baby: Unfortunately, breast cancer and maternity patients are on the same floor in the Women's Pavilion.

"No, my wife just had a mastectomy." And I can hear Tyler's voice drop.

The resident checks out my pump and tells me it has been blocked for hours—no pain meds for all that time. What the hell is wrong with my husband? It is the first signal that he should not give me any medical advice. He is a knee doctor, not a boob doctor and I am his wife, not his patient. Why is he so insensitive to my pain? He tries to make it up to me the next day by bringing me sushi for dinner. The sushi is so soft and does not hurt my chest when I chew it.

I spend the next day, my first day without my breast, in bed. Everything hurts. It hurts when I breathe in to smell a beautiful bouquet of red roses. It hurts when my friends sit on the corner of my bed to be near me. It hurts especially when I need to roll over to pee in my bedpan. When I take a sip of fresh-squeezed carrot juice to help get my energy level back up, I feel the wound beginning to ooze.

I get some good news: my lymph nodes are clean. I have never seen my parents so happy. They are jumping up and down and hugging the nurse and it looks like they are in a Megabucks Lotto commercial. Clean lymph nodes...the things we took for granted before this happened. The nurse reminds me that my right arm will be very prone to infection because I do not have lymph nodes anymore on that side. No blood drawn on that side, no blood pressure on that side, and no manicures. I know I will cheat. I can't walk around with just my left hand polished. I am already going to be missing my right boob and I'll need other things to match.

The next day I am determined to be glamorous for my visitors. I will not pee in the bedpan. It takes me about twenty minutes to get out of bed, still attached to my IV pole, without moving the drains and tugging on the stitches holding together my skin. I do manage to pee on the toilet but I can't reach to wipe and need to call a nurse. I ask her to help me put on my white waffle cotton robe—it bulges slightly but fits over the quart-sized plastic drains that look like milk cartons. And I take out my jewelry bag. I knew I wouldn't be able to take a shower after my surgery because my wound would have tape all around it and wouldn't be able to get wet. Since my hair would be greasy I brought jewelry to make up for it. I decide to wear my freshwater-pearl chandelier earrings because the white looks nice with the white cotton robe. And it matches my bandage.

As if on cue, three dozen perfect, creamy white roses arrive in my room. "Thinking of you, Barbara Walters."

My mom, dad, and brothers do not leave my bed. My mother-in-law Marie, my father-in-law Gerald, my sister-in-law Leslie, my Uncle Marty, Uncle Steve, Aunt Marilyn, Aunt Pamela, Uncle Bernard, Aunt Nancy are all there. My friend Suzanne makes sure that I have fresh doughnuts every morning. My friends sit on my bed until the staff tells them they have to leave because visiting hours are over. They answer my phone and laugh: "Geralyn Lucas's room, how can we help you?"

But when my gynecologist—the one I first showed my lump to—comes to visit me, her visit reminds me of the sadness of where my life left off.

"Geralyn, I am so sorry this happened. Please don't get pregnant. It will be too dangerous for you now."

I need to see Dr. B's face to feel some hope. He told me that I will get my life back, that it will be a hard year, but then things will return to normal. Dr. B is supposed to come see me today and I need to look my best for him. He will probably feel guilty to see me in so much pain, knowing he has cut off my breast. But I feel a strange closeness with him, since he has cut me open and stitched me back together. I can't reach to brush my hair—it would pull the stitches too much. I can still tilt my face down to apply my lipstick. But I can't reach my arm up to curl my middle finger and make the perfect lipstick arch between my lips. It would hurt my drain stitching too much.

When Dr. B arrives he immediately clears the room and sits down softly on the corner of my bed. He must know after performing so many surgeries how much a little bed pressure can hurt a wound.

"Geri, wow you look like you're feeling well."

It is quiet and the only noise is the beeping of my pulse monitor. It starts to quicken because I know what he is about to say.

"Have you looked yet?"

"I can't."

He walks to the door and locks it. He walks over to the bed and pushes the white waffle bathrobe to the side and opens my blue surgical gown and his face drops a little because he sees what I feel: fresh blood seeping though the gauze.

"Don't move—you need to have this dressing changed and we're going to take a look."

I turn away and close my eyes again. I have been closing my eyes every time a nurse, a doctor has changed the dressing.

Dr. B is wiping off my wound, asking if it hurts, telling me that he is almost ready for me to open my eyes. I remember all the times I opened my eyes when I was little, anticipating surprises—wonderful presents. I try to imagine what I will look like and Dr. B answered my question:

"Geri, open your eyes. You look beautiful. It's okay."

Before I open my eyes I remember the bizarre photo album in the office of my plastic surgeon. Dr. P was the last doctor I went to see before I decided that I could have my mastectomy. Her photo album convinced me that I could do it. I had needed to see what it was going to look like.

She is an expert in breast reconstruction after a mastectomy. She took out a photo album unlike any photo album I had ever seen: disembodied torsos of reconstructed breasts. Really, they looked like mug shots of breasts—bad lighting and the breasts looked so serious, like they knew they were posing for a reconstruction photo album. They looked better than I thought reconstructed breasts might look, I guess, but just so much blankness where the nipples should have been. And that was when I realized that having a mastectomy meant having my nipple removed as well as my breast. No one had told me that part.

A breast without a nipple? It just wasn't right. Like a pizza without pepperoni, a cake without icing, a sundae without a cherry on top. Dr. P must have read my mind and kept flipping the pages until we arrived at some tight shots of nipples. I am confused but she explains that she made those nipples. Nipple tattoos. She folded skin on the reconstructed mound to make a little pucker and then tattooed it a nipple color.

I think I was even more surprised when Tyler told me that there's a doctor at Mount Sinai who is famous for his nipples. Strange specialty. Especially when introducing oneself at a cocktail party. But now I was relieved that there were experts in this type of thing. Maybe I could be whole again. Maybe I could get a fabulous reconstructed breast and even a nipple. Maybe I could pass.

Dr. P explained that there were choices on how to build my new boob: traditional implants or a tummy tuck where stomach fat was used to build a new breast. (After some serious pinching Dr. P told me I didn't qualify because I was too skinny.) Another option involved a "donation" from another part of the body. The only fat source I had was on my butt and yes, that was where she would take it from. How strange. If I was going to lose my breast, why would I want to lose my ass, too? I still want to be a piece of ass. It just didn't make sense. Especially after I asked what my ass would look like after the donation? There was even a photo in the book to show what that looked like: like a shark bite.

Dr. P told me that she would insert a special breast implant called an expander when my breast was removed. It is a temporary one, a place holder boob that she will keep blowing up with fluid to stretch the skin so that when she switches in a regular implant my skin will slope and look like a natural breast.

I was just so relieved that there would be a mound there when I woke up.

After I saw Dr. P, I needed to ask Tyler what would happen to my breast after it was cut off of me in the OR. Would it just be thrown away? Would my nipple end up in some garbage dump somewhere? Tyler reassured me it would be refrigerated in a pathology lab, and somehow the idea of my nipple in some large refrigerator in a Tupperware container marked "Lucas-nipple" was an odd comfort. He probably made this up and I am so grateful. Like a kid who needs to believe in Santa, I need to believe my nipple is not just being thrown away.

But now I will see the reconstruction results on me and not in that breast book. Dr. B has finished removing the dressing and he's begging me to look. "Geri, come on, open your eyes."

When I open my eyes all I can see on my chest is a bright red line that looks like I took a Sharpie indelible marker and drew a diagonal line exactly where my right breast used to be. There are stitches that look like black spiders climbing up the red line, and except for the red line down the middle, it is a regular smooth skin mound that sort of looks like a breast mound. I try to remember what had been there only days before but I can't.

I think about the Tupperware to calm myself down. Dr. B and I look at each other. I just nod and I feel relief that the curtain has been pulled away. Dr. B readjusts the bandages and tapes them back over my mound. No more hiding. No more mystery. This is my new breast.

Now I need to show Tyler.

After five days in the hospital, they send me home with the plastic drains still sewn into my chest. I need to keep emptying them every few hours and keep measuring the fluid coming out to make sure that I am not bleeding too much. I want to leave the house, but I don't own any shirt that fits over these milk quart–sized plastic containers. Tyler lends me his Tulane sweatshirt and I put on some lipstick and finally leave the house for a sushi dinner with my parents. It feels so good to be out of the hospital and to eat my dinner off of Japanese pottery instead of a plastic tray and plastic containers. But every bite of food and every swallow feels like it is pulling the milk quarts down on my chest and pulling my skin, and what would happen if my drains fell out in my favorite Japanese restaurant?

Tyler has not seen my chest yet. But tonight when he gets out of the hospital he is going to snip the milk quarts out of me so that I don't need to visit my plastic surgeon for that part—after all, he did a breast cancer rotation during his training.

It will be the first time he has seen my breast after my mastectomy. It is so humiliating that this will be his first look. I want to be able to clean it up for him first, dress it up a little. But it's hard to find a negligee that will fit over the milk quarts. My hair is greasy, too, because I still can't take a shower and get the dressing wet. What will he think when he sees this? I know he has seen a mastectomy before in his training, but he has never seen it on his wife.

Tyler is concentrating so hard when he is snipping the stitches off my chest that I can't tell if he is shocked or just in surgeon mode. It is still raw and burns. The strangest part is that I can't feel his hand moving along my new breast as he is snipping. There is no sensation. I am trying to remember what the nipple felt like there, when it used to feel so good.

I don't know what to expect. It is almost like a doctor-patient moment and it feels very professional. He finishes snipping the especially hard pieces of string, caked with my blood, that have kept the milk quarts on my chest.

When he finishes he puts the scissors down and wipes off the wound. He is looking in my eyes and I notice that his eyes have changed from a medical, surgical look to an "I want you" look. Tyler smirks and his hands have moved from my wound. I notice that I have started to bleed a little where the stitches were. Tyler does not miss a beat.

"Geralyn, let me put on a fresh bandage so we can have sex."

I need to put on some lipstick.

7

Cocktails

When I see the IV bag with a skull and crossbones on it wheeling towards me I realize that I am actually about to get poisoned. I am sweating as my oncologist, Dr. O, begins to explain the chemo "cocktail" the nurse is about to push through my veins. But I finally hear a word I can hang on to in this white sanitary place: *cocktail!*

A strange thought pops into my head: When was the last time I was actually at a bar drinking a cocktail? I could really use a very dirty martini, Absolut vodka, extra olives on the side, right about now to help my courage kick in.

Funny, I was never daring in the cocktail department. I was president of Students Against Driving Drunk in high school. I never had a fake ID. A Sea Breeze was as cool as I got. I could never say "Sex on the Beach" or "Orgasm" with a serious face to a bartender. Now I'm having a poisonous cocktail.

First day of school, first kiss, and now first chemo. I'm not sure what the dress code is for first chemo, I mean I know this is not a time for appearances, but I do want to look good facing this assault. I have worn lipstick and my favorite crimson suit because I have just come from *20/20*. I am also wearing the beautiful antique Murano glass necklace that Tyler gave me the night before my mastectomy. One of the glass globes is pinkish red, and it highlights the crimson of my suit and the red of my lipstick perfectly.

Tyler can not be here because he has to be at the hospital with his patients. So my mom has taken the day off from her job as an elementary school guidance counselor to come with me to my first chemo. My mom used to love telling me that my first word was *out*. I'd stand in my crib and point and say "out." Right now I would do anything to get the hell out of here.

I am being so mean to my mom that it's reminding me of when I was in high school and I took out all my frustrations and anxieties on her. The other patients keep shooting me nasty looks like, "Be nice to your poor mother—look at the hell she is already going through and you being snotty is making it worse for her." My mom is being so cool, just there as my pincushion as I am about to get this huge needle.

Dr. O has ordered me a deliberately deadly cocktail called CMF: cytoxin, methyltrexate, and 5FU Fluorocuracil. Cytoxin means cell killing. After I hear that, I figure out that the methyltrexate and 5FU are chasers. Maybe like sucking a lime after a tequila shot, I try to reassure myself. And there are more cocktails. It feels like Unhappy Hour: a steroid cocktail to manage my body's reaction to the poison and an anti-nausea cocktail to control the vomiting and diarrhea. It will not work, but it will blimp me up fifteen pounds. The anti-nausea cocktail makes me vomit and they try another concoction on me. Instead of Zofran I get Kytrol, which is a cousin of Zofran. Are whiskey and bourbon cousins or somehow related?

I ordered the CMF instead of the AC (adriamyacin, cytoxin) because the doctors told me that although the adriamyacin was stronger, it could cause heart failure. That scared me, but it feels frivolous to worry about a little heart failure when the goal is to kill all the fastest-growing cells in my body.

I think about how the frat guys I went to college with used to chug beers and put strange tubes down their throat to get the maximum amount of liquor into their bloodstreams in the shortest amount of time. Why not just use an IV? I guess because IVs are too serious. There is something really wrong when an IV is involved. Basically because they follow you everywhere—there's no getting away from them, especially when you badly need to pee. I learned how to walk slightly ahead of the pole so I could look more elegant when I had visitors in the hospital, but it is still a ball and chain. There are too many IV poles rolling around this oncology office.

The skull and crossbones on the IV bag means poison, and the poison is about to go inside my vein. It is going to kill *all* of my fast-growing cells because it can't find just the cancer. So that is why my hair will fall out, my stomach will cramp, and my white blood cell count will drop, making me exhausted and prone to infection. My veins will turn black, singed from the poison shooting through them, until they look like stripes against my still very white skin. I will look like a heroin addict. Whoever thought of heroin chic never had heroin veins. I will pull my sleeves down and never wear my favorite black dress because it is sleeveless.

My chemo nurse, Nurse C, introduces herself. How does she look so happy in this place? Even the way she snaps on her rubber gloves seems playful. Everything about her does not match the chemo room—her huge blue-green eyes, her fiery red hair, and her large earrings—except for her white nurse shoes and white nurse's uniform. When Nurse C rolls the IV pole towards me, I remember that I passed out at my high school blood drive. I didn't even have the needle in me yet.

I have been training myself with the hypnosis for this needle especially, for my chemo shots. I don't pass out when I smell the alcohol or when they tie the rubber band around my arm to make the vein bulge or when they make me clench my fist around a rubber ball. But I am sweating and starting to see black dots. I tell the nurse that I might faint and she has a glass of OJ and a hard candy for me to suck on. I try my mantra: "I am like the sky and nothing can stick to me."

The needle feels like it is pulling on my vein and then I feel the rush of the cocktail being forced through it. It feels like it might burst, it is so tight and hard and cold. I did not order my CMF on the rocks. "Nurse this feels really cold."

She grabs a blanket to cover me and my mom tries to hug me to keep me warm. I am pushing her away to show that I can handle it. But I can't. I am so scared that I'm at the beginning of the marathon because I have only just started the poison. There are so many patients in the same chemo room who look like they'll barely hobble to the finish line. Is that where I am headed?

The needle stays in my arm and the pushing goes on for hours and it feels like there is a brick balancing on my tiny brave vein. I am trying to read *The National Enquirer* to take my mind off my vein. With my right hand I'm eating a chocolate Entenmann's doughnut to get the strange metallic taste out of my mouth that they warned me about. I can't move my left hand because it has the IV taped securely to the top of my hand. They have started with the vein in my hand to preserve the other veins for future treat-ments. What feels like forever and a lot of cold pushing later, when Nurse C finally removes the needle from my relieved vein, Dr. O wants to see me in her office.

I chose Dr. O to be my oncologist because she reminded me of Glenda the Good Witch. Even though she doses out poison, there is a fairylike quality to her. She probably wishes she had a magic wand under her white coat, because there are so many sick people in her office. Dr. O is a woman you want on your side when shit is going down. When she talks it is like she is petting you. "Geralyn, your first chemo was wonderful. Your white count looks beautiful. Why not go home and relax and order in a movie and dinner with Tyler?"

I feel so unsteady when I leave her office, like I have drunk way too many margaritas. My mom needs to put me into a taxi before she hails her own cab to get downtown to the train station. I am scared that I won't make it the twenty-three blocks uptown with-out puking.

When the empty taxi pulls over the first thing I hear is heavy metal music. I mouth "no" to my mom—I do not want to step into a Black Sabbath concert now because I feel so queasy. My mom sees how sick I am and wants to ride uptown with me but I know if she does she'll miss her train. Anyway, I need to prove that I can take a fucking taxi and I'm not dead yet.

I kiss my mom good-bye. She has already paid the cab driver and told him that I'm not feeling well, please drive carefully. Even though my mom and dad grew up in New York, they act like such tourists, way too friendly to people. I've told them not to say hi to people when they walk into elevators. It's a giveaway they are from out of town. She is talking too much to the cab driver now. I need to take some control.

"Sir, I'm going to Ninety-sixth and Park."

What am I thinking? He's covered in tattoos and wearing a black bandana and I just called him "sir"? Chemo must already be affecting my brain. "I just had my first chemotherapy treatment. Please, please try to drive slowly. I'm so scared that I'll vomit in your car."

The next thing I hear is soft classical music and he has pulled his taxi over. Oh, no. Another taxi moment because I have cancer-confessed. "My wife had ovarian cancer and it was the chemo that nearly killed her." He rolls down the windows in case I need to vomit and drives so slowly that we get honked at four times. He actually parks the taxi in front of my apartment building and insists on carrying my bag and walking me to the front door.

I am so optimistic that I order Indian food (maybe that will get the metal taste out of my mouth) and tell Tyler to rent a movie just like Dr. O told me to. I want to be a good patient. The problem is just that I can't get off my bathroom floor. This cocktail leaves me feeling worse than a notorious night I spent leaning over the toilet swearing I would never drink another cocktail. I am vomiting and shitting at the same time and I am so covered that I need to peel off my clothing and throw away my favorite crimson skirt. I will never wear that suit again.

I can't believe that I need to go back to that room and have another cocktail.

I decide for my next chemo I need to have a cocktail party in my chemo lounge. It is catered with McDonald's, Entenmann's chocolate doughnuts, and lots of other things to get the metal taste out of my mouth. I invite my parents, brothers, Aunt Lynda, and friends. My chemo contingent is taking up about half of the chemo room where all the patients sit and get their cocktails. They take turns holding my right hand. How are they so brave? My dad tells me that he would take the shot for me and I know he means it.

There is something about the chemo room that makes us all feel close and honest. It is more intense than sitting at a bar to have a cocktail and getting so drunk that we say things that we've never said before, more intense than sweating in a sauna together. The chemo room is about realizing everything we have ever taken for granted, especially not having cancer. We've all looked around and realized how short life could be. My family and friends make chemo fun and take me out to EJ's Luncheonette afterwards and then on a little shopping spree. No matter how tired I am from the chemo, I always have a little energy left to shop and eat, even though everything I've been eating lately tastes like a rusty nail. I have started craving strange things like macaroni and cheese and mashed potatoes with gravy all mixed together.

It's so jarring to go from the chemo room back to normal life. When I return to my job and hear my coworkers complaining that they've gotten a minute cut out of their story and they are in full panic mode, I can't relate at all. Maybe a visit to the chemo room would make them understand how lucky they are.

The next few cocktails build up in my bloodstream and now I am totally tanked. I lose control of my bowels in a taxi. It is not really my fault. I couldn't warn him because he's on his cell phone and not speaking English. He keeps hitting the brakes really hard, and each time I think I am holding my sphincter muscle as tightly as I can—but he caught me off guard when he slammed on the brakes at the red light at the intersection of 81st and Central Park West.

I am so drunk and off kilter. Even carrying a newspaper feels heavy.

I will vomit every day for the six months of chemotherapy. I have systems: I have learned to steal vomit bags from airplanes. If you ask the stewardess she will usually bring you an entire handful because she is scared you're going to heave at any moment. I carry those bags everywhere. I also carry a change of clothing, in a vomit-proof plastic bag, of course (I quickly learn that supermarket bags leak). And I figure out which dry cleaners will deal with vomit and still smile when I come to pick up my clothing. I carry around a tin hairspray aerosol that I spray every time I vomit in the ladies room at work so my colleagues will not know that I've just spent an hour on the floor. Most important, I carry around a hankie doused in Poison perfume—like they did in Victorian times—to offset any offensive smells that could trigger vomiting. I learned my lesson after I stepped into an ATM that a homeless person had slept in all night. My only misfire was a dog. That was tricky.

As my veins turn black, my stomach convulses, and my skin turns green, I cannot begin to imagine what must be happening to my eggs. I think my nest is unraveling and it is under attack. I can't order eggs for breakfast anymore. Scrambled, over easy, it's all torture. Especially fried—that's what I fear is happening to my precious eggs after the chemotherapy poison. When I feel a menstrual cramp I am convinced it's a chemo cramp. When I start to bleed again I am convinced that it's just another bodily fluid oozing out of me. But when the blood continues, I know my egg is okay. It has somehow survived this assault. I continue to bleed. I was never one of those women who felt it was womanly. It just bummed me out that I couldn't wear my white satin pants and that I still felt paranoid getting into a swimming pool. Now, each month my blood is a telegram from my eggs: "Still kicking!"

The chemo begins to have another strange side effect; this one no one warned me about. I become so tired that it feels like I'm watching my life in fast forward on the VCR. Why is everyone speaking so fast, moving so fast? I need to regroup on the sidewalk and sit down because it hurts to hold my hand up in the air to hail a taxi. Taxis don't even stop for me anymore. Maybe they can't see me hailing as hard as I used to. But I know it is really because my skin is green, I am bloated, and my hair is starting to fall out.

I begin to blur and I start to disappear.

I never realized how often men used to look at me on the street until they stop. I would give anything for a once-over. It's as if I don't exist. I just walk by as an invisible woman. I suddenly don't count.

I remember when I counted. When men would smile and even catcall and when the men at the coffee counter would make a point of asking me if I wanted sugar in my coffee just to extend the conversation. Now, I am looked through on the coffee line. They take *her* order before mine even though I was on line first. They never ask if I want sugar. No eye contact.

I decide to stop wearing lipstick. I am too tired to remember to put it on, and no one is looking anyway. And one day it happens. "I" completely disappear.

If you don't believe me, I even have a picture to prove it.

I have to get my photo ID taken at ABC News. My luck they

decide to change the security system now. Everyone needs to get a new ID picture. There is no chemo waiver.

My friends are headed over to get their picture taken and are waiting for me at my cubicle.

"I have to return this call," I lie, because I need to be alone to face the camera.

I wait until the end of the day to walk down the long corridor towards the security department. There is a little mirror in the security station where the photos are being taken. I guess it's a courtesy thing for people to make sure they like the way their hair looks. I do not even look. I am avoiding mirrors. Anything shiny or reflective makes me scared. After I caught a glimpse of myself in the microwave pantry at work, I have become more careful.

My hair has really started to thin.

I have learned to blow-dry my thinning hair with my eyes closed. I never blow-dried. Now, I try to do anything to fluff the hair that is hanging on until the next cocktail. It is a strange form of self-deception.

The security man knows there is something wrong with me because my skin is so green from my last chemo treatment. I start explaining. I tell him about the chemotherapy I have been taking and how my hair is falling out. He has an idea. He turns on the fan in his office. It is October and already slightly chilly. He is trying to create the windblown look on my thinning mane. I am so grateful for the fan. It is an act of random kindness. It makes me smile when I see the flash of the red light. But even my smile is not the same.

I place the ABC new photo ID in my wallet and it is directly across from my Columbia University ID card from just a year ago.

That Geralyn is gone: the thick long shiny black hair, the the-future-is-mine smile. The lush eyebrows! I look over at my new picture: I am swollen and my skin has a sallow, green tinge.

My oncologist had warned me that my hair would "release" from my chemo. Releasing is just a very fancy word for falling out. I had never really noticed her hair until we had this conversation during a consult about which chemo I should have. Her hair is the color of Campbell's tomato soup (with cream added instead of the traditional can of water). It is wavy and a perfect bouffant shape of mini ocean whitecaps all over her head. I think she wears hairspray (so I know she must care about her hairdo, too). Her hairspray is not the kind that makes it stiff, but the kind that keeps her looking perfectly put together while she is consoling a patient and telling her her white counts look "beautiful." She was noticing my long hair.

"Geralyn, some women are more comfortable losing their hair if it's shorter. Why not cut your hair so it's easier when it starts releasing?" She must see my apprehension and offers Plan B.

"Some women even shave their hair off beforehand so they don't need to worry about it falling out."

"No way, I can't."

"I think you should get a wig and have it just in case." Dr. O is still looking at my hair.

8

Hair Removal

Losing my hair is harder than losing my breast because everyone can see it happening.

And "releasing" sounds so more elegant than it actually is. The word should be "shedding." I am like a shaggy dog because I leave hair everywhere I go. I leave my hair on chairs during important meetings at work, on clothing I try on in stores, and at friends' apartments. It is so embarrassing and it feels like everyone can actually see me unraveling. Long black strands of my hair are on my pillow, on my *New York Times*, on my kitchen table, and all over my hardwood floors. I secretly collect it so that people will not notice all the hair I am leaving behind. I can't believe how much hair I must have had, because there is still so much on my head even though so much has fallen out.

Wax, tweezers, Nair, razors, shaving cream, Jolene bleach are all products of my recent past, kept on a hopeful shelf in a medicine cabinet. Thinking of all the time and money I spent removing "unwanted" hair makes me wish for it all back. Well, some of it anyway. Just enough to cover this small bald patch on the top of my head that people can't help but stare at. I remember when I used to get other kinds of stares.

It is an ironic time of year for my hair to be falling out. It is autumn, and everywhere I walk, there are leaves falling from trees. Autumn used to be my favorite season, but now those naked branches are so sad to look at.

I take Dr. O's advice and decide I need a wig. I do my research and I find the most high-end wig salon in New York City. Saying the word "wig" is just too crass here. When I walk in a young man comes up to me and runs his fingers through my hair. He is caressing my hair, actually. I wonder if when he is touching it any of it will just fall out in his hands. He starts to smell it and asks me what type of hair products I use. He must have a hair fetish and he clearly found the right occupation.

His boss comes over, brushes him aside, and asks me if I am here to sell my hair. I must look really confused because then he asks me if I want to buy extensions—maybe on closer inspection he has noticed the balding spot on the top.

"I started chemo and I started releasing and I need to get a wig."

The younger man hugs me and starts to cry. A real boo-hoo sniffle cry. The older man tells him to pull himself together and gives me a stroke on my face and tells me to follow him. There are a lot of men dressed in drag in the shop trying on long blond wigs and I realize it is only a week before Halloween. That makes my being here seem crueler. I am buying a real costume, a wig I will need to wear every day just to pass, and they are just having fun playing dress-up for a night of partying.

The younger man is trying to pull himself together and his eyes are still red and his lip is still quivering. He touches my hair again, gently, for a texture feel, then brings over two Styrofoam heads with straight black hair and bangs on them.

"These are real hair wigs and very expensive. Women in China sell their hair for dowries." He explains to me that this particular wig took four women's impending marriages to be made, as he pulls the wig over my head and instructs me on how to glue it on. So that's how wigs stay on? Glue? The hair is almost identical to mine. Long, straight, and black. The bangs are exactly the same. I look at myself in the mirror. The wig looks the same as my old hair except that the wig seems thicker.

I always hated my hair. The kids in elementary school used to chase me around the playground and call me witch because it was so long and black. My hair was always my signature, though. When my three-year-old neighbor drew a picture of me, there was long black crayon scribble. And if any witnesses were to describe me at a crime scene, I am sure "long black hair" would be the first words they would use. Now I am feeling guilty that I ever hated my hair. It is so beautiful, how can I lose it?

I put the wig on hold and leave the store. I am wig waffling. I keep going back to try it on, putting it on hold, going back, and not buying it. But this is not like putting a sweater on hold, and they are losing their patience with me even though I know they feel badly for me because I have cancer. I need help and I ask my boss Meredith to come with me to help me pick it out. Meredith is so classy and has such great taste and is always brutally honest about what she doesn't like. Forget "does my butt look big in this?" I am now dealing with "does this wig look okay?" and I really need someone I trust to pick out my hair.

When I return with Meredith, they pull out the wig, and several men gather around, saying how beautiful and natural the wig looks. Meredith does like it, but she thinks it needs a better haircut to look more natural. But there is nothing natural about cutting off your hair for a dowry. I cannot let that go. They are instructing me about how to wash it, and then suggesting another wig, too, a more casual one that is only half real hair. I can even wash it in the washing machine. The older man has come over to whisper a secret: "You need to get your hair cut. It's too long and it's releasing and it's such a mess."

He is touching my hair again and his moist eyes are convincing me this is something I need to do. But how can I get a haircut when it is all about to fall out? He tells me the salon next door specializes in this type of haircut. He walks me next door and introduces me to Gabor of Salon Gabor. The man from the wig shop tells Gabor I need a "haircut."

I tell Gabor to please not cut off a lot, just a trim, and he understands how reluctant I am to remove anything, considering the circumstances. I am praying he will not cut off too much since we both know it is not going to grow back anytime soon. As he is snipping and the hair is falling around me I start to cry because this is not a normal haircut. There is just nothing normal about my life these days. It is not normal that all I worry about is living until I am thirty, putting my eggs in a safety deposit box, and proving myself to my bosses at ABC not because I'm a recent hire but because

I want to show them having cancer doesn't mean I can't be counted on.

Gabor cuts me an I'm-about-to-totally-lose-my-hair-from-chemo-so-I-need-to-get-a-few-inches-off-so-it-won't-be-messy-when-I-really-lose-it shoulder-length bob. It is sweet how it flips up on the ends and he tells me how pretty I look. For a moment I even forget about my little bald spot.

But I begin releasing so much that now I am down to combing over the patches of hair on my head. Every time the wind blows, I panic. I thought I would start wearing the wig but when I try it on all I can see is how wrong it looks on me. I squint my eyes and the hair comes into focus, and that is when I think maybe I can see them: the women in China. They are lining up to cut off their hair so they can get a dowry. Giving something away because they have to.

Maybe I purchased their courage? The wig feels like a cover-up and I'm pretty sure I don't want to hide my baldness. I'm scared everyone will look at me and know I'm wearing a wig. I guess I really want everyone to really see me and understand what this cancer is doing to me. I decide I will not wear the wig, and that I want to go bald, slowly. I remember the women in China. I have to be brave.

It takes all the courage in China to leave my apartment when I am officially a comb-over. I have always wondered why any man would ever wear a comb-over. Now I know. My comb-over is screaming that I can't let go. I am holding on to those defiant pieces. I am begging them to stay put—no, ordering them to hang on, please pretty please. I refuse to let anyone trim them, those few combed-over patches (even comb-overs need a trim). I have become like one of those comb-over men because I will not let anyone near it.

People notice me on the street and then quickly lower their eyes. But they look up again. They are rubbernecking and I am the car wreck. They must wonder what is wrong with me and I think that is good. I want them to notice what breast cancer has done to me. I think about the other things that I had tried to cover up, like zits in high school. I want this flaw to get noticed.

I miss my ponytail most. It used to be a my-hair-is-such-a-mess-I-will-just-pull-it-back ponytail. Now, a ponytail seems like such a luxury. So much hair that it needs to be tied back? I can't remember that. A ponytail seems like such a trophy of health and so carefree, and will I ever have a ponytail again just wagging back and forth like a happy dog's tail?

Shampoo commercials seem to always be on. I watch and drool: the one where the woman flips her hair in slow motion and then they kind of freeze when she flips her hair back. That extended moment of hair glory is too much. It is hair porno. Way too hard core, nothing subtle about these commercials.

I start watching Hair Club for Men infomercials at 3 A.M. when Tyler is on call at the hospital. I cry during the testimonials, when the men talk about how different they were before they lost their hair. How confident they were, how happy they were, successful they were. I understand. When they get their new hair, they seem like they are really existing again, not just wearing hairpieces. I almost order that spray paint stuff that they sell for bald spots on another network. Almost.

When I get to L.A. on assignment (to convince a woman who left her husband and daughters to marry a convicted killer in jail, to tell her story) I panic because it seems harder to be a balding woman in L.A. where there is so much gorgeous hair (and breasts). No one can see my one boob in L.A., but my balding head is obvious. Being a bald man in L.A. is sexy, but being a bald woman is different. Someone must be looking out for me, though, because I get to fly first class. Dr. O insisted because she said the air is much purer up front and all the recycled air could make me sick because my immune system is so compromised. It is really embarrassing to explain my situation to ABC Corporate Travel and I even have to get a doctor's note.

When I am in L.A., all I see is hair, most of it blonde. The camerawoman I'm working with finally asks me if I'm okay. I can't help but notice her beautiful blonde shoulder-length hair. "Oh, I'm going through chemo and I don't want to wear a wig."

She is so sweet and concerned and asks why I'm not wearing a wig. I am not sure why until I'm at the airport coming back to New York I see a young man with one leg. He has a metal rod for the other. I know about the rod because he is wearing a pair of jeans and he has deliberately cut one of the pant legs short. I understand why he is showing it and maybe I understand my decision to show my balding head more. I want people to know that I am suffering and how invisible I feel.

But I am not invisible in Dr. O's office because I look too young. This is not the kind of getting noticed I am craving. When a nurse says "Mrs. Lucas" during one of my consultations with doctors everyone expects my mother to be the patient. She is in her fifties like most of the breast cancer patients. One patient makes a point of telling me in great detail one day that my case is a tragedy.

"I thought what was happening to me was cruel. And then I saw you. How old are you? Twenty-something? Unbelievable tragedy. At my age I guess I expected this, but you . . ."

Is that supposed to make me feel better? Are there lesser evils here? I need to be invisible here, too.

I guess I want everyone to notice my baldness except my mom. Today she is coming to take me to my chemo. The last time she saw me was two weeks ago when I was still releasing, but now I am balding. I am scared for her to see my baldness. I don't want her to be scared of how I look. Maybe I will wear the wig for her. But maybe seeing me in a wig would break her, too.

Before my mom picks me up in the taxi at *20/20* to take me to chemo, I consider putting on the wig—I have it and the wig glue in my bag. I even considered calling her and asking her not to come, but I need her there. Having her with me at all these medical appointments is so much better than having her with me at a Girl Scout troop meeting when I was little. When I step into the taxi, my mom touches my head.

"Oh, Geralyn, your hair is really coming out."

I can see what this is doing to my mom. I am going to glue on that wig, I'm thinking to myself. But what she says next stops me from ever wanting to wear the wig again.

"You look so courageous. I'm so proud you're my daughter."

I have finally found a way to get noticed again.

But it is so short lived. There is one more rambunctious release left that makes even my comb-over fall out. I am in the shower, and when I start lathering my comb-over, most of it stays in my hands. The big patches of hair just come out. No warning. It is there in my hands with the shampoo lather. I calmly rinse off the suds and place the hair in the sink outside the shower. In a strange way, it reminds me of my first haircut lock, in my baby book, tied with a pink bow. I dry the chunks of hair that have just fallen out and put them in a Ziploc bag. For some strange reason I need to save them so I can touch them and see them if I need to. I can't just throw them in the trash.

I have thrown too much away lately.

9

Meeting My Mojo

Now that my hair is gone I realize, standing in front of the mirror looking at my baldish head, that I might have nothing left to lose. Since the past has betrayed me and the future is uncertain, my life is all about "right this minute." I need to live up to every moment. Although I am disappearing on the outside, what is left inside feels so raw and powerful it's hanging on with claws screaming, "My show must go on! Don't give up now!"

I need to find a way to walk out the door and show up at work bald.

I bought the black wool baseball cap as an experiment to see if

I could wear it instead of a wig. When I put it on, I can't see out from underneath it, so I turn it around and it looks kind of cool.

I am not cool. I wore pink monogrammed sweaters in high school, and my style is still conservative: Jackie O suits, bangs with shoulder-length hair. I have had the same hairdo since I was two years old. I am reluctant to take fashion chances. But my life has now become about taking chances, because I might be dying and time is so short so what do I really have to lose?

So I put on my favorite black suit to match the baseball cap, but it still doesn't really match because the reverse-style baseball cap is too cool for my black suit but it will have to work because I need to leave the house. My doorman touches his hat as he holds the door for me. He must notice my cap.

I am so scared for everyone at *20/20* to see my baseball cap because they will know that my hair has finally fallen out. Is it disrespectful and unprofessional to wear a baseball cap to work? I called my boss Meredith to ask if she thought it seemed rude of me to wear the cap to the office. She told me that I was being ridiculous and of course I should wear my cap.

On my way in the door at ABC News, I wonder if the security guard notices my cap. Getting into the elevator and riding all the way to the tenth floor is testing my strength. By floor 8 I am thinking about hitting LOBBY again but it is too late and the doors open at 10. I see the landing. It is a runway, waiting for me to show off my new cap and also show the office that my hair is officially gone.

As I am taking a deep breath, I see my executive producer, Victor. I was hoping to make it to my cubicle before anyone could see me so that I could reposition my cap one more time. And I was hoping I could test it out on some other coworkers before the big cheese saw me with it. I am praying that he doesn't notice my hat. Since my cancer, all I want him to notice is my work.

I haven't missed a day of work since I returned from my mastectomy surgery. It was hard to come back because it felt like everyone was talking too fast. My chest was also pounding, but I refused to take my painkillers because they made me too tired. I keep coming to work. Showing up at work defines me. Just being there is a victory. I am too scared to lie at home in bed because I feel like I am dying. I need to prove that my brain is still working. It is really all that I have. Even on the day when there was twenty-six inches of snow on the ground, three buses, two vomits, one subway, one taxi, and four treks over huge piles of plowed snow later, I showed up. I rested once, but who even knew that. All that mattered was that I was there at my cubicle, ready to pounce on the day's top stories for 20/20.

My stomach is cramping, my hair is falling out, but at least I can still think. My brain is on fire. I can't count on anything else in my body but my mind. I am bloated, I am seasick, I taste metal, my right eye keeps tearing, but I still am finding great stories for 20/20 segments. No one on the other end of the phone knows I am bald. Part of my job is to deliver newspapers, and lately I've had to deliver one at a time because they feel so heavy. I don't tell anyone.

And controlling my body has become a constant challenge. Every day I will myself to make it up the ten floors in the elevator without puking. It would be so humiliating if I didn't make it and vomited on Hugh and Barbara. I mean, they're my idols!

I am on my chemo for two weeks, and then there is a two-week break. For the two weeks straight that I am "on" chemo, I take a cytoxin pill six times a day. No wonder cytoxin means "cell-killing," because about twenty minutes after I take it I feel my stomach cramp and I need to go into the bathroom and just deep-breathe or puke and then spray aeresole hairspray to cover the smell (not as obvious as air freshener). It is stressful having only a cubicle during such privacy-demanding moments, but thankfully, my cube is right next to the bathroom. I am a frequent visitor. I always show up at work on Friday afternoons after my chemo shots, too, even though my skin is the shade of an artichoke.

My skin color and thinning hair aren't the only things my bosses are noticing. I am convinced that everyone at ABC only knows me as "cancer girl," especially because I was profiled in an ABC News special called "Cancer in the Family." But when I get paged to Victor's office, Meredith is there waiting, and they want to promote me! I am just hoping to live out the year, but they give me a three-year contract. They believe I will make it, and they don't want NBC or CBS to hire me away. Getting noticed at work is giving me some power back and pushing me to be bolder and turn up the volume in my life.

And now, even today, after all my hair has just fallen out in the shower, I am here. *My show must go on.* But facing Victor in my baseball cap feels almost as hard as when I told him that I had cancer. I keep my eyes down and try to keep walking, but he stops me.

"Geralyn! You look so cool! I love that hat!"

I am stunned by his compliment, and so grateful that Victor can see my coolness and not my cancer. I *am* reappearing. I am still tired all the time, but especially tired of looking so exhausted and feeling invisible. I think I have found a way to start reappearing. I am holding on to myself so hard while things are falling away. How do I explain this power?

I remember a little food shack in Provincetown where I used to spend my summers when I was little. It was called Mojos, and it was painted all different colors. When the wind blew I heard chimes floating in the air. I can still picture the way the word *Mojo* was written in wavy letters. I thought I knew what *mojo* meant—but I wasn't sure. I kept asking people. Everyone knew what it was, but couldn't explain it. The word *mojo* is now popping into my head all the time. It feels so mysterious. I look it up in the dictionary to make sure my mojo is the real thing. Pronunciation: 'mō-(,)jō. A magic spell, hex, or charm; broadly: magical power.

I have cast a spell over my own life. I have willed myself to find my magic that must still be there. Despite the baldness and one boob and occasional heave, I am charming. I have met my mojo.

Things that used to scare me don't anymore. Cancer scares me, people don't. I can ride in the elevator with Barbara Walters and not be scared of chitchat. There is suddenly something so free about living in the moment. How do I feel so alive while all of my fast-growing cells are being killed in chemo?

Mojo.

My mojo keeps pushing me to reappear.

Cancer is making me cooler than I have ever been. I dare myself. Every chemo treatment, I wear a shorter skirt. I had always loved showing my arms and their definition from the weights at the gym, but now they are covered with black veins. I decide to show leg instead. My tailor keeps blushing as I direct him to go even higher above my knee. I start wearing high heels to chemo, too. Hearing the click of my patent leather strappy shoes against the sanitary white floor gives me so much hope.

The shorter skirts are making my cap look more deliberate, but they still do not match. I buy a black satin miniskirt and a black satin cap to match. It looks deliberate and the cap is blending and it doesn't seem like just a prop to cover my bald head. The dress

code at ABC News is working—someone in the elevator is startled
to hear that I have cancer.

"I always thought you were just downtown. The hat and short
skirts?"

Downtown seems so far away from my uptown doctor offices
and the chemo that I just smirk. Downtown?

I am wearing tighter sweaters to match my short skirts. The expander boob implant my plastic surgeon put inside of me is really
too big to fit into my tailored suit jackets. It is also bigger than my
left breast, so I need to even myself out with a falsie on the left
side. I realize that my boobs don't really look even in anything I
wear except tight sweaters. I think the tightness and gravity pushes
them together and down and makes them look sort of similar—
maybe it is an optical illusion? I always wanted big boobs—maybe
I should be careful what I wish for. How crazy that I have breast
cancer, but my boobs are getting more attention. Every time I get a
stare I want to explain that they aren't real, but then I realize how
needy I feel for attention, any attention, and I decide to take it. I
am thinking that everyone at work must be checking out my ever-
changing rack even if they don't mean to. I know it's true when
the cutest producer on staff pulls me aside one day and confirms
my suspicion.

"Geralyn, you look really good."

"Thanks." I am so glad that I started wearing concealer to cover
the green tinge of my skin from the chemo.

"No, you look really, really good," he says, and stares at my
boobs for a second to make his point.

It is so high maintenance to keep pulling this off. Instead of
asking my friends, "Does this make me look fat?" I am always asking if my boobs look even in the shirt I'm wearing, and if there are

enough stray wisps creeping out of my baseball cap, and if my skin looks too green.

It is not only my style that is changing, it is my substance. Somehow, losing my breast and hair have made me more daring, which has made me more seductive and even sexier. Living with the risk of dying is making me more and more and more risqué. Every time something goes, I try and amp up something else. It's a distraction technique designed to thoroughly confuse the viewer, and it's working. I have found some inner cleavage I never knew was there. It keeps daring me to keep going.

I unplug my juicer, which is filled with parsnips and beets and wheat grass. My parents convinced me to eat macrobiotic when I was diagnosed and I have been juicing every day and trying to eat seaweed. I had a consult with a health guru who told me that caffeine, sugar, and alcohol make the tumor grow. But those are all my favorite food groups, and since I have been eating a special health diet I hold my nose through most meals. I decide to throw out every piece of tofu and seaweed from my refrigerator, and I order a bacon-egg-and-cheese on a roll with a large coffee on the side. If my life is short, I need to taste it now. Mojo.

And when I feel my mojo waning, I borrow some from my boss, Meredith. Mojo is Meredith's middle name. I always seem to be strong at work, but one day I pretend that I need her advice about a story I am working on, but when my butt hits her sofa, I sob.

"Meredith, I'm so tired. I'm so scared. I can't take the chemo anymore. I feel like I'm dead already."

Meredith locked her door and blocked all her calls, even though the broadcast was the following day, and hugged me for what felt like an hour. My mojo is returning.

I dance the Macarena at our office Christmas party. Mojo.

I hire a personal trainer named Hakim and tell him I need to make sure I don't lose my range of motion after my mastectomy surgery.

"Hakim, please push me hard. I know I'm going through chemo but I can handle it. I need to work on my legs because I've started wearing shorter skirts."

"And oh, could my butt ever look like yours?" Mojo.

On the anniversary of our engagement I want to be romantic and sexy for Tyler, but my mouth tastes like metal from the chemo and I really do have a headache (and a stomachache). I can't find any lingerie that fits over my two different-sized boobs and I don't want to wear the baseball cap to bed. I am feeling so not sexy it is ridiculous. I want to him to touch me so badly, but my chest still hurts from my mastectomy surgery. Actually, everything hurts.

I consider putting on the wig and tight sweater with the falsie inside my bra—maybe I could have sex with Tyler almost fully dressed? I wish I could have sex with my clothes on. I want to hide but I also want to just be there totally with Tyler, like we used to, in the bed. I have been sleeping with a beret so Tyler doesn't have to see me bald. And I've been wearing a bra with the falsie even under my nightgown just to reassure myself that I sort of match.

I put on some perfume. And I line my lips with lipstick. I can't even feel Tyler's hand when he puts it on the bright red diagonal scar across my chest. In fact, I have been walking into strangers with my reconstructed right boob because I cannot feel where it starts.

But the great thing about sex is that it's like riding a bicycle. I know that Tyler still loves me—my laugh, our conversations—but will he still be turned on?

Yes, yes, and definitely yes. I cannot believe that Tyler wants me so much.

The way he is kissing me and touching me, I know that it's not my hair or my boob that ever made him fall in love with me. It was my mojo. It was always there, just waiting for me to meet it.

After Tyler and I have sex again I feel so hot that I still can't get that Shania Twain song out of my head: *Man, I feel like a woman!*

Mojo.

10

Busted!

The invitation to my ten-year high school reunion arrives just as the last substantial wisps of my hair have fallen out and there is almost nothing peeking out of my baseball cap. Besides my baldness, I am more worried that if I go to the reunion my classmates will notice my boob job. It is obvious.

I had been an A-cup in high school. As in lots of A's. I was smart—or always tried hard to be. A goody girl, that's what my brothers called me. Now I was a D-cup. As in Duh! Something has changed!

I know that I seem conceited thinking everyone will stare at my new rack. Although there are only two letters between A and D, there are a lot of stares. B—boy, she changed! C—can't be real, she must have had a boob job. I could reveal the reason for my boob job before they judged the cover of my book—double D. I have been going through breast cancer reconstruction, and it is obvious.

I never understood why they called it breast reconstruction until I went to my first appointment to have my implant "expanded." I should have worn a hard hat. Expanding is a polite way of saying that your plastic surgeon is going to pull your skin so hard that you'll want to scream "motherfucker!" as loud as you can.

My plastic surgeon, Dr. P, takes a needle to locate my "port" switch inside the implant, and then fills my implant with so much saline solution that my skin stretches like a balloon about to burst. Can skin burst? I think my new boob is going to explode right there in her pristine Park Avenue plastic surgery office. I imagine bits of my skin and implant flying around the room and landing on her diploma. It hurts and presses against my ribcage. I must have gained five pounds from all that saline! The night after my first of four expansion procedure "blow-ups" I make up my mind. It is 4 A.M. and I am pacing the hallway of my one-bedroom apartment. Tyler is on call at the hospital. I am taking another Tylenol with codeine because my chest is pounding from being so overinflated. I am worried that all my expensive suit jackets that I bought when I got my job at *20/20* won't fit over my new rack.

But I decide that if it hurts this much to rebuild my breast, I am going to hurt to look at. My breasts will have to be large, round, and worth the hell I am going through. At my next expansion I tell Dr. P to bring it on, blow me up, and please make me look like *Baywatch*. I am going to get some cleavage out of this. Thankfully, she has never seen *Baywatch*. I try to explain the idea of it—big, gigantic, fake, implant boobs.

"Geralyn, my work is natural. When we're finished I want you to look like you have *not* had work done. You're a petite girl and I just can't make your breasts that large." I reluctantly agree and resign myself to having tasteful breast implants. Reluctantly. If my breasts might kill me, then I want them to stop traffic.

The hardest part about reconstruction is finding a bra that fits. My left breast is still an A, but my right construction site is a double D from all the inflating. I have had to find a falsie to pad the left real boob so it matches my right side. My chest always looks like it is sloping down on the left side (thank god assymetrical shirts are in!). To further complicate things, I only have one nipple, so when I get a headlight there is just one, which is so obvious. I need padding so my left nipple doesn't show. I cannot believe the little luxuries that I used to take for granted. Like wearing a bathing suit: Now the falsie just floats around once the water creeps in. My seven-year-old cousin Alissa had to hold her towel up for me as a shield when we went swimming together recently. She knew I was nervous that the falsie was on the loose. What would happen if my falsie went wild at my high school reunion? That would be memorable.

Yes, I have a good reason to skip my reunion. Actually two: I am missing my hair and a breast. But I need to show up because I am scared that I will not live to attend the next one. I need to be accounted for. Even if they whisper my fate and the C-word in ten years, at least I can be here now.

My life has become about showing up, because if I die I won't have a chance to. It's a way of proving to myself that I am still alive. Showing-Up Syndrome started with going to my friend's wedding in Sun Valley, Idaho, even though it was only one day after my first chemo. After I spent the night vomiting on my bathroom floor, I had to get on a plane—I had promised her I would. Tyler thought I was crazy and wanted me to stay in bed. He thought it was ridiculous to fly out Saturday morning and fly back Sunday night because it was such a long flight to Idaho. On the way to the airport, the cab driver asked what airline we wanted, and that is when I saw the signs announcing which airline was located in which terminal. *Terminal.* I had not heard the word since my diagnosis and I started to shake and sweat. *Terminal.* Please, please, please do not let me be terminal.

But I couldn't tell Tyler how scared I was because he was grumpy the entire flight. To add to his bad mood, we had a mechanical failure and were diverted to Atlanta. My life felt like one big mechanical failure. I, too, am experiencing engine trouble. When we finally arrived at the wedding, we had already missed the ceremony and most of the party, but I did get to see my friend in her gorgeous Vera Wang wedding dress being skated around the ice rink on a chair by her hockey-playing groom and his groomsmen. I got my picture taken with the bride and I felt I had accomplished my mission because I was somehow there. I will be in her photo album. Even if I die, my picture will be there.

On our return flight, when we landed, I was so scared to face the *Terminal* sign again. And there was more bad news blaring in our terminal on CNN airport televisions. Linda McCartney had just died of breast cancer. I had been obsessing about dying anyway, but this news put me over the edge. How could someone that healthy (Linda was a vegetarian), that fierce, that rich die of cancer? If anyone could have "beaten" cancer, Linda McCartney could. I was starting to realize that cancer plays by its own rules.

That is why I need to show up at my reunion—I need to be accounted for today because I might not be here tomorrow. But I definitely don't want to tell everyone from high school that I have breast cancer. That I am in treatment, doing chemotherapy, and undergoing reconstructive surgery. I am embarrassed. I still feel like a freak for being so young and having breast cancer, and it is mortifying to have to say the word *breast* to people I have not seen since high school—how immature is that?

I also need an escape now. Everyone at work knows and I have basically become the Cancer Girl. I am nostalgic for the me before the cancer. And, I am also being practical: I am not sure my high school class can handle it. My high school class was high school shallow. The cool kids did drugs and were pretty mean to the smart kids, who studied and were pretty mean to each other because they weren't cool. Do I trust revealing my cancer to this group? Have they grown up? Will they pity me? Will they look at me with the are-you-going-to-die question mark on their face?

And there are logistical considerations. Will I need to tell the whole story again and again or will it spread like a virus after one person is infected with the gossip? Geralyn has cancer—other people have a baby, a husband, a big job, a red Porsche. It feels cruel and unfair. I know that I have accomplished so much more than a cancer diagnosis, but how will they know? Cancer is the headline. Anything else I say will get lost.

My high school class voted me Most Likely to Succeed. I was managing editor of my high school paper, *The Merionite*. That was high school, but my life has gone on, too, even though it is stalled right now. I graduated from U of P and Columbia Journalism School. I'm married to a smart and good-looking doctor. I'm a producer at ABC News. I am convincing myself that I am not only a cancer diagnosis, and that I deserve to be more at my reunion.

I decide that I will reveal to my classmates the truth that they hadn't seen in high school: I have become cool. But I'm scared of getting caught. I'm scared they will realize that I am hiding my cancer.

To pull off my ruse, I need to keep dressing the part of my new cancer chic. I call my friend Rebecca and explain my dilemma to her: I need to find a shirt that is really daring, but also makes my boobs look even. So many of the shirts I have been wearing make me look uneven. I am sloping downwards on the left side, too high on the right. Rebecca becomes my accomplice and tells me to meet her at Bloomingdale's. We find a chocolate-brown satin shirt. The shiny texture surprisingly covers the bump from my falsie nicely. My boobs just look big and firm. There is no plastic Jell-O jiggle from my falsie when I walk because we also bought an 18 Hour support bra (I always wondered who needed those things). I pick a brown suede baseball cap and stacked brown men's shoes. I wear extra-tight khakis and I tie a sweater around my waist for effect. Rebecca is totally into the stylist role and even tries to trim the straggly micro-wisps that peek out from under my baseball cap.

I am an imposter, scared of being caught and judged. Isn't that so high school of me?

I can tell I've put on too much makeup when I see my reflection in the mirror behind the bar after I walk into the restaurant in the Philadelphia suburbs on the night of the reunion. That wasn't part of the cool plan—it's just that my skin is really green from the chemo. I have never pencilled in my eyebrows before—but they, too, have thinned, and now I realize I've made them too dramatic. But wait, this *is* dramatic. This is *Terms of Endearment*, *Steel Magnolias*, and I could be up for a Golden Globe.

I have only two co-conspirators in the room, my closest friends attending, Jessie and Julie, who have been so supportive since I was diagnosed. I smile at them and know my plan is working when Randy tells me he had a crush on me in seventh grade. Rob can't stop staring at my new rack and is suddenly interested in me even though he never seemed that interested when we spent an entire year together on the student government executive committee. He suddenly wants to know all about my life.

C for cool is going smoothly. Tyler is in the room and I feel like I'm showing him off like a trophy because in high school I always thought that guys weren't interested enough in me. I was too smart, too serious, and maybe my boobs were too small?

No one is even suspicious that I'm not having a drink: In high school I was president and founder of a Students Against Driving Drunk chapter. A few classmates are teasing me that I still don't drink. (If they only knew about my chemo cocktails.)

I am giddy and I've forgotten that C is for something else until I see Ted. He sat behind me in homeroom for four years. He always hid my pocketbook. He picks up with the lame flirting where we left off ten years ago.

He is teasing me. "You think you're so cool—so bad. You live in New York, look at your hat!"

Suddenly, he is reaching for my hat.

"Stop! Ted! I have cancer, I have no hair under this."

A drama is unfolding. He is crying and fleeing to the bathroom, and two girls follow. My cover is blown. I need to get out of there quickly. I run over to Tyler and Jessie and Julie and tell them that I need to go because I'm exhausted, and I am. I am not sure if it's the chemo or the energy I've put into being such a faker.

When I say good-bye to Jessie and Julie I don't know how to thank them. Despite all the high school drama we lived through together, I love Jessie and Julie most for being there with me tonight. For supporting my decision to fake it and never judging me. Tyler did not understand why it was so important to me to fake it, and he really wanted no part in it. He just stayed in the corner with Jessie and Julie's husbands. I wish he had understood and had stayed by my side, held my hand, been my co-conspirator. He is always curious about why I even care about what other people think. I think if he had been me he would have walked into that room and told everyone. But I just couldn't admit what was happening to me.

I am so exhausted from the reunion that I cannot even eat Thanksgiving dinner when I get back to my parents' house where I grew up. My mom and dad and family friends are there and everyone wants to ask me about the reunion. All I can think about is a nap. But once I am in bed upstairs, I feel so disconnected, like pretending at my reunion that I don't have cancer. Showing-Up-Syndrome is starting to feel so shallow.

I am in my old bedroom, still painted yellow with all the yellow fake country French furniture from my childhood. Under my blankets with my hat still on in the dark and cold, I hear everyone downstairs, singing "Happy Birthday" to our family friend, the song I'm so scared of now.

The sounds of "Happy Birthday" are just hanging there in the darkness. I hate that song so much now because it is reminding me that I might not live. That I had to have a mastectomy a day after my birthday. And now I feel that life is happening without me already. It's like I already died. I always wondered how my family would be without me. Would my brothers be okay? Would my parents drown in their grief? I am relieved that they can go on, but selfishly, I want there to be sadness downstairs, too. I feel like a ghost in my own life. Why am I even trying to be a part of things when I am not really even here?

But I am not the only one feeling strange. My mom tells me the next day that everyone was crying when they were singing "Happy Birthday." It was not happy, because I had cancer. And a few of my classmates called who had been at the reunion to see if I was okay—they must have heard that I was sick.

Despite being "caught," I am still glad that I went to the reunion. No matter what anyone else in the room had accomplished—how big her house was, how much money he made—I realized I had earned the title my classmates had given me: Most Likely to Succeed. Just because I showed up. In that room I felt the sadness of my life now, smacked up against all the promise I had thought it held.

I never thought I would get cancer. Especially not when I was only seventeen years old and about to graduate from high school and the world was waiting for me. I thought I would do great things.

I knew now that in a strange way I had.

Everything about me seemed different now because of the cancer, but some things had remained exactly the same.

11

18-Hour Support Bra

The first thing I think when I wake up after my implant surgery is that I have a newfound respect for strippers. This hurts soooo much.

After four blow-ups in my plastic surgeon's office, I have reached the final phase of my reconstruction, which involves a surgery to replace the reconstruction expander implant with a real saline implant. I have also decided to get an "enhancement" implant on the left side to match the new bigger fake boob on the right. During my intake at the hospital, the nurse seems to be very rude to me.

"Have you had any other surgery?" she asks.

"I had a mastectomy in August."

Her face drops and she actually says she is sorry and I realize she thought that I was just another one of those silly plastic surgery junkies checking in to have a boob job. Well, sort of.

They send me home with drains stitched inside of me again and I empty my drains all night. I am pretty used to what the wound fluid should look like after wearing the milk-carton drains so often after surgery, but this time it looks like pure blood. Tyler comes home from his hospital shift at midnight, and when I show him the blood he mumbles that I should probably go to the emergency room and then passes out from exhaustion.

When I call Dr. P the next morning she is panicked and I am rushed into emergency surgery because I am bleeding where my new implant is. I am too scared of the drama to feel angry at Tyler for blowing me off last night. He has been so sleep-deprived from his surgery residency and taking care of me during the night shifts at home. It is so hard for him to be on-call for me, too.

On the way into the operating room I am thinking how crazy it would be if my breast implant killed me and not the breast cancer. Am I vain to be going through this?

After the surgery they check me into Tyler's orthopedic floor in the hospital. He's on call so if I'm on his floor he can see me tonight. Tonight, I just want to be one of his patients, not his wife. I want my bandage to be on my knee and not my boob so that he can change my bandage and reassure me. I want him to care about my cancer the way he cares about his patients. One of his bosses comes to my hospital room and hands Tyler a textbook and a video and tells him that he is doing a hip revision surgery tomorrow . . . another patient is pulling him away.

But even after all that expanding my skin is still not sloping naturally enough and it is pushing the reconstruction implant too high up on my right side. So like all construction projects, we are over time and over budget. I need another surgery to move the implant lower down. Dr. P is working so hard to make my now reconstructed boob perfect and I do appreciate what a perfectionist she is because I do not want to be lopsided in my new tight, tight sweaters.

After my final fix-it reconstruction surgery there is a beautiful gift waiting for me, a box wrapped in beautiful ribbons and tissue paper, from a fancy lingerie store. It is from Meredith. I open up the box and smell lavender, and underneath the tissue paper is a gorgeous see-through white lace bra with satin loops stitched all around the borders. When I take it out and hold it up to my chest, I realize how out of place and ridiculous it will look over the plastic drains with the wound fluid accumulating, over the red Sharpie line, and over the jagged stitches. I feel like Cinderella covered in rags and ashes but still dreaming of wearing a ball gown and glass slippers.

I decide that this nippleless mound, this implant, this stretched skin will someday deserve to wear a lacy bra, too. This beautiful bra has given me hope and somehow showed my boob its future. I remember the pictures of the nipple in the photo book and I think that as soon as this scar is healed, as soon as these drains are pulled out of me, I am getting my new nipple, and putting on this bra.

Meredith's gorgeous bra makes me realize that I need to trade in my 18 Hour support bra, throw away my falsie, and find a bra that fits because my boobs are finally even—well, the most even they have been in a long time, after the last surgery. I now have matching implants on both sides so I do not need to keep wearing the falsie, the plastic chicken cutlet–feeling fake boob that I have been using on my real boob to match the expansions. The falsie has become part of me; if it's not on my body it is sleeping beside me in its plastic holder.

I finally get to remove the plastic pup tent that's been over the wound for weeks. And it hurts. I don't want Tyler to touch it because I just cannot summon any sexiness. I have not showered and I still smell like the hospital. I take a shower and try to wash the hospital smell off of me and my new breasts. It is finally time to throw out the falsie and my 18 Hour support bra. They have been my crutches through this whole experience.

Reluctantly I go to Victoria's Secret. I feel like an imposter, shopping like a normal woman in a bra store—my agenda is so much more complex than most women's here. I am trying to imagine what kind of bra they all need: a strapless bra for their sister's wedding, a foxy bra for their new boyfriend, a cream-colored bra for their new white cashmere sweater. I just need a make-me-look-normal bra. Do they sell those here? I am trying to pass as a regular woman even though I only have one real boob. Each table I walk by is boasting the best-fitting bra to push me up, contour me, even perform a miracle for me. Victoria's Secret doesn't know how badly I need a miracle. I only want to look even—at this point I would call that a small miracle—and I can't have anything too sheer because my one nipple might get hard, and it would then be obvious that I have only one. I also need to hide my scar, so nothing see-through because it is still a bright red diagonal bolt across my new breast.

I have no idea what size bra I wear now, and I am slightly intimidated by the saleswomen with tape measures around their necks patrolling the store. As I'm fingering a lacy black bra and wondering what it would look like over my scar, I catch a glimpse of the tape measure coming closer, closer, and closer. I can practically see the lines of the inches. Oh no.

"Can I help you?"

The saleswoman seems too confident. She does not realize the challenge she is in for. That tape measure has never measured this kind of measurement.

"I'm not sure," I stammer back, terrified of that tape measure.

"What type of bra are you looking for? Have you tried our new miracle bra?"

"I just need a bra that fits. I am not really sure what my size is. . . ."

"Most women are wearing the wrong bra size. Most sizing issues are purely psychological." The saleswoman seems amused that I think I am alone in this predicament.

I take a deep breath and I get it all off my chest. "I used to be a 32 A, then I was a 34 double D on my right side only because I had a mastectomy and my skin was being stretched with an expander implant so that my real implant would slope naturally, and I just got an implant on my left side to make it match but my right side is still higher on my chest . . ."

Oops. Too much information. Cancer confession. I remember my poor deli guy and every other innocent bystander I have blurted to.

The saleswoman has not even missed a beat. "What size are you wearing now, dear?"

"Oh, this. This is my 18-Hour support bra. I don't even remember the size."

Rebecca had found the perfect 18-Hour support bra to help me get through my reunion. But it had done more than help me pass. The support bra had supported me in every way. Just knowing how strong that bra was, knowing that it could endure for eighteen hours and that it had promised to give me a lift. I never understood why any woman would need eighteen-hour support. Now I know. I needed it so badly lately. *Support.* Actually saying the word *support* is having a strange effect on me. Thinking that I need to trade in this support bra is making me weak.

The saleswoman opens a dressing room with her key and puts her tape measure around my chest. I feel like a science project. I had started out with my original 32-A-cup bras and I busted out after my plastic surgeon expanded my reconstruction implant. When I tried to even myself out on the other side, the falsie never seemed to fit inside the other cup. I must have moved up to the D's at the height of the construction, which is when I bought my support bra, but now I am swimming in it as she pulls the tape measure tighter.

"You're a 34 B!" she announces with tremendous authority.

I must look like I doubt her, but I'm just amazed that my boobs can be anywhere near a normal, regular size? It feels so much more complicated: the cancer, the expansion, the scar, and the one nipple. How did all of that become a standard bra size that I can try on in the Victoria's Secret dressing room? Although technically I have only gone up one bra size from before I had cancer, there were saline and stitches and stretches and so much sadness in between that I haven't been sure what to expect. As my boobs were being blown up with saline, my heart has been stretching in all different directions, too. It hurts.

I cannot give up my support bra.

The saleswoman leaves my support bra and me in the room and returns with several black lace bras. I cannot take the support bra off.

"Dear, can I help you with that? It's really the wrong size."

I feel slightly dizzy. I sit down on the bench in the dressing room. The thought of taking off the support bra is making me physically ill. The word *support* is echoing through this tiny, fluorescent-lit cage. The pretty pink-striped wallpaper is reminding me that buying bras should be a sexy experience, but now it's causing me psychological trauma. It is reminding me of everything wrong with my life lately. Of all the emotions and people that I have been avoiding because I have been trying to survive my chemo, my surgeries, and my job.

"It's my husband," I stammer. "I'm scared I'm losing him."

The saleswoman does not seem fazed by this confession. I keep going.

"And my mom, I'm so worried about her. We're Jewish and she has become a Christian Scientist! I don't think she can handle the idea of me dying. She needs to believe my body can heal itself.

"My father doesn't cry around me, but I heard that he broke down sobbing while presenting at a board meeting."

The saleslady goes to put the black lacy bra on the little hanger in the dressing room. I'm not sure if she was planning to hug me or if she just accidentally brushed up against me when she was reaching, but now we are embracing with one push up, one miracle, and one smooth-as-skin (and my support bra) between us.

I tell her everything.

Before this moment I haven't told anyone that I felt Tyler was slipping away from me during my cancer treatments. All I wanted was for him to acknowledge that he was scared that I might die, but he was always insisting that I was cured and ended any conversation I wanted to have about what would happen if my cancer came back and if I died. Whenever I said how scared I was, or how uncertain my future felt, he usually cut me off: "You're cured." I knew it was supportive that he believed that I was cured, but I wanted him to worry with me.

But, maybe I had pushed him away?

Maybe I was so scared of dying on him that I decided to leave him anyway.

Would I always be his wife if I died? Would he marry someone else?

What would happen if I disappeared?

I needed to know. Robin was in my bed with me last night after I had just vomited for the ninth time that day. I tried to eat a cheeseburger but now it was all over my toilet. I brushed my teeth and started to cry.

"Rob, you will always be my best friend. Even if I die. Will I always be yours?"

"Ger, you are not going to die."

"If I do, you can marry Tyler."

"What? Ger, what are you talking about?"

I had been working on a story at *20/20* called second chances. It was about a couple who got married after their spouses had both died of cancer. They met and fell in love in a support group. I wanted Rob and Tyler and everyone in my life to have a second chance if I disappeared. But, I also needed to feel irreplaceable. I want to know I will still be part of my life, even if I die. But, I miss Tyler now.

I had thought it would be too much to ask for to expect a husband who was compassionate and who would hold my hand at every chemo appointment, but I saw the other husbands in the chemo room. I had a different idea of romance now—it is not chocolate, roses, perfume. Romance is holding back your wife's thinning hair while she pukes so hard that she pees in her pants. The whole chemo room was a love song, except for me. I felt more like a country music song. The lyrics would be something like, "First I lost my boob, then I lost my hair, and now I've lost my husband."

A lot of insensitive people had told me every story they'd heard about husbands leaving wives with breast cancer. The implication was that I should feel lucky that Tyler was sticking around. And everyone was treating me like I should feel so relieved that I was already married, the implication being that a one-boobed girl definitely could not get laid. I would prove them wrong.

In fact, I had even drafted a singles ad:

One-boobed woman with extra-large heart seeking companion to share chemo treatments, bone scans, and surgery recovery. Ability to handle vomiting a must. Sperm donor also wanted in near future. Non-smokers preferred.

I had assumed that hanging out in hospitals might be appealing to a doctor. But it wasn't. Tyler didn't have the time to come with me to most of my treatments because he was always on call at the hospital. And he didn't understand why I needed people there with me at my treatments. He thought that I should just be "mature" and go on my own. I guess the last place he wants to be when he has any spare time is a hospital. He is in the hospital day and night. And the last thing he wants is a patient in pain at home, because he is treating patients in pain all the time.

I was so jealous when I saw the other husbands in the chemo room at my last treatment. Tyler had shown up once, but he missed my last chemo treatment. That was the one that I needed him to be at most. I thought the last time would be a relief and that I would be so happy to walk out of that oncology office with a Band-Aid on my poor bruised vein, so relieved I would not have to come back for another shot. But it was the first time that I cried in the chemo room. I finally let myself feel the prick of the needle and take in all the sadness around me. I couldn't before, because I had to keep coming back. All my friends were there, my brothers Paul and Howard, and my parents, taking turns holding my hand and hugging me. My parents had arrived separately. My cancer had even complicated their thirty-year marriage. There had been a snowstorm and my mom had refused to drive from Philly to New York because the roads were so dangerous. She took the train because there was no way she was missing my last treatment. My dad wanted to drive because he thought that way he could control getting to my treatment on time. He always thinks he is sturdier than a train, and I think he would have walked the one hundred miles if he'd had to.

Even though there was a ton of beautiful white snow in New York for my last chemo, Tyler was in Aspen skiing. I had had to postpone one of my chemo treatments because I had a low white count, and he had a ski trip planned for this date. He didn't cancel it. I thought he should be there with me to mark the end of this chapter. I thought he was trying to tell me that his life would not pause for me, that it was business as usual. I knew that Tyler was just being practical and he definitely needed a break from his hospital job and the cancer ward at home. He didn't think that the last chemo was any different from the other chemos, but I thought it was very symbolic. To me, it was an end, and a beginning, and I needed to know that he understood this.

Tyler had tried in his own way to be supportive during most of my chemo. One night he went out to find me apple pie à la mode and Apple Jax at midnight when I was having chemo cravings. Chemo would do that to me, make me crave anything I saw advertised on TV and make me crave food I had not eaten since I was in second grade. Tyler also bought me a beautiful antique lamp to keep by my bed on the nights he was on call so that I wouldn't be scared (he knew that I was still afraid of the dark but was too embarrassed to use a nightlight).

When I talked to Tyler about how I wanted him there for me more, he rolled his eyes.

"Why do you need anyone else there for you? There's a mob of people around you at all times. I can't take it anymore. Why does it even matter if I'm there at all? You have everyone else."

Was he trying to force me to choose between him and my family and friends? Did he feel lost in the crowd?

As I was losing part of Tyler, I started to realize how much my family was there for me. I needed my mommy and daddy more than ever, even though I was twenty-eight.

To celebrate my last chemo my parents planned a surprise party for me at the Top of the Sixes building in New York City. It was very glamorous: there was champagne and veal chops and delicious chocolate cake. I try to taste everything and I even swirl a tiny mouthful of champagne around in my mouth. I think I can taste the future, except for the metallic film in my mouth from the earlier chemo cocktail in Dr. O's office. We are all seated at a long white table clothed table surrounded by huge windows overlooking New York City covered in white snowflakes. It feels like we are inside a plastic snow globe that is being shaken hard.

"All I want for my birthday is what I already have."

That is my dad's toast to me. He breaks down and starts to hug me so hard. It is his birthday tomorrow. My ending chemo is his present. I was so relieved to finally see my dad cry. I had asked my mom why Daddy never cried about my cancer. It really bothered me because he is so sweet and sentimental about everything: a walking Hallmark card.

"Geralyn, Daddy cries all the time to me. All the time. He wants to be strong for you."

When my mom told me that, it made me realize how hard it has been for all of their lives to go on while mine is unraveling. My poor younger brothers: How has Howard found time to come to every chemo and still study for his law school finals? How has Paul had the energy to call all my friends after every surgery to let them know that everything was okay and still try to make partner? How has everyone been able to be so supportive of me?

Meredith also made me an end-of-chemo recovery party. I was overwhelmed at my *20/20* party and didn't know how I could ever thank them enough for believing in me, for promoting me during my chemo, for accepting me with my ever-changing boob sizes and my hat and short skirts, and counting on me more even though I might die. Barbara Walters handed me a beautiful bouquet of flowers at the party, "Geralyn. How are your parents? Give them these from me." I realize that they have been my eighteen-hour support bra, pushing me up every hour of my day, giving me that lift always.

Here now in the Victoria's Secret dressing room I need to remember all of their support. I know why I'm scared to trade in my support bra. Everything has changed, especially my boobs. So how can I ever wear a normal bra again? Will I ever be normal again?

I thought about what the saleswoman had said about wearing the wrong bra size. She was insistent that most sizing mishaps are purely psychological. She explained that some women are still wearing the same bra size as when they first developed. And others are aspiring to be a certain size but can't fill it out. I realized that she was right. I needed to trade in my support bra and to adjust to my real new size. I have had to adjust to so much. We have all had to adjust.

With some Kleenex and prodding from the saleswoman I take off the 18 Hour support bra. It's a relief not to feel that sturdy firm material pushing so hard against my breasts. But can my boobs fit into a normal bra?

The miracle bra lives up to its name. I have two awesome mounds of curves. The padding even hides my scar. When I look in the mirror I can't believe what I'm seeing. It fits perfectly! But the strangest thing is, I finally have cleavage! I never had cleavage—I was always too flat. But my plastic surgeon has fixed that. You go girl!

The saleswoman is so proud of her work. This might be the best fitting bra that she has ever sold. I needed to take some credit, too. It had been quite a journey to find the perfect fit.

It feels strangely appropriate to gain some cleavage after everything my boobs have been through, and to have my breasts look hot in this bra. With all my supporters pushing me up, holding me up, propping me up, there was no way my boobs were not going to stand straight up now.

And along my journey, I had definitely discovered my inner cleavage.

It was finally starting to show.

12

Falsie

My new bra is daring me to show off my new cleavage. But I have become so used to being invisible that I am not quite sure how to reappear.

I put on the bra and buy a tight red low-cut shirt. I am getting lots of stares but I feel sort of guilty. Is it false advertising? Is it somehow wrong to want to flaunt my breasts after breast cancer?

I throw away my falsie. It is reminding me of my past, and when I touch the hard gel I feel the support it has given me through so much. It has been a prop I've used to continue in my life and keep going during so many weak moments. It has become like brushing my teeth. Every morning, I popped my falsie into my left bra cup. But I don't need it now.

And there are more changes. My black veins are starting to fade since I drank my last cocktail. My hair is starting to sprout back. I was convinced I would be the first woman to never have her hair grow back after the chemo. I couldn't even imagine when I lost it that it would really grow back.

But I cannot let go of the few long hairs that have clung on throughout the entire ordeal. Those remaining hairs under my baseball cap have become some sort of strange security blanket. I am reluctant to get any of my long hairs cut. My friend Suzanne makes me. She is a lawyer who specializes in extraordinary ability, and she has a client who has gained his citizenship because he is an extraordinary hairdresser. But can he handle this challenge? I am not convinced there is enough new hair to even cut. And I do not want him to touch the long hairs—they cannot even be trimmed. They have been loyal to me and I still might need them.

When I arrive to see Thomas, the extraordinary hairdresser, I am too nervous to take my baseball cap off. Since my hair has fallen out, I have even been sleeping with a hat on. Suzanne is there to help me. She has even paid for my first haircut as an end-of-chemo present. Suzanne and Thomas are begging me to take the baseball cap off and I feel like a man holding on tight to his toupee. This cap has been so loyal to me, it feels like it's become part of me. What will I look like without it?

When I finally do remove the cap, Thomas is intrigued. There is so much more hair there than any of us realized. He explains to me that there is the "old" hair and the "new" hair and it all needs to be cut to the same length. This is an extraordinary situation and he does seem to know what he is talking about. This haircut is reminding me of the I'm-about-to-lose-my-hair haircut. I guess this one is the I'm-about-to-get-it-back cut. Haircuts never used to be this complicated. It is so crazy that I am the girl who never even liked getting trims.

Thomas starts to cut and I'm surprised that it takes him as much time as it does. The result is shocking. Suzanne is screaming.

"No way, no way! Look at yourself!"

Lucky for me that buzz cuts are suddenly in style because that is exactly what I have. A very micro crew cut. It is so spiky and all my hairs are standing straight up.

Thomas shows me how I can wear scarves over the cut, and how to put hair products in. Suzanne gives me her scarf to wear out. I tie it over my head and make a knot at the nape of my neck. Tres chic! I am going to meet my family for brunch and I realize that my hair will be shorter than my brother Howard's buzz cut. It is unfortunate that I am wearing my black leather jacket because I now look too tough. When I stop someone on the street to ask directions, I realize that my voice does not match my haircut—it's too high and sweet. I need to lower it. I need to start living up to this haircut.

My family is so impressed and thankful to Suzanne for making me lose the wisps and the hat. It was about time to come out. My brothers and my dad convince me to take off the scarf. But I feel naked. When I show up at work with my new haircut, I have Suzanne's scarf tied around my head to hide how short it is.

"Take off that rag." One of my friends at work wants me to strut a little. I take it off and get a lot of stares and compliments.

"Wow—where did you get that haircut?" Women on the street are stopping me now. I give too much information and just blurt about the chemo but they really just want to know who cut it. *Self* magazine even features my new haircut in a "Radical Cuts" article. Meredith leaves an article from *Vogue* magazine on my desk. "Buzz Cuts Are a Must!" Thank god.

If I was unsure if I was back, I'm not unsure for long; men are looking at me again and letting me know.

"Hey, baby. Nice hooters."

My boobs are starting to get a lot of attention and it feels as fake as the saline implants inside of them. But somehow, I have earned these cheers. I deserve this attention. I convince myself that if they really knew what I looked like under my bra, what I had gone through to get this cleavage, they would be howling, too. I have earned every *wow*. But I am so deeply reluctant to inhabit this new body. I am used to counting only on my mojo. I feel strange getting attention from what is on the outside because I now know how quickly it can leave with no warning. Over the past few months I have found another way to exist and I refuse to get attention from my boobs and hair now.

I really want to disappear now that I have become visible again. I am hiding at work. I know that I should be flaunting my new look, my new energy, but it all feels so false. I cannot believe that any of it is here to stay. I cannot get attached to any of it, because I am convinced that my cancer is going to come back any day. I do not want to get too used to not having an IV pole in my arm. I do not want to be normal again if I need to have more chemo and surgery. I still might die.

And I have developed a new phobia: I am scared of waiting. My Uncle Steve and his daughter, Alissa, took me to Disney World when I finished my chemo. The lines for the rides were forty minutes each. I would start to sweat and panic. I cannot wait on line at the ATM machine. When I speak to my therapist about my fear, it becomes pretty clear. I have waited too long in waiting rooms for bad news. I feel I have no time to wait! I cannot wait for anything more in my life, I can't wait at all now because I think that I am dying. I am so scared because I have stopped the chemo. I am certain that the cancer has started growing in my body again.

Aunt Honey, my mom's best friend, calls me when she hears about my waiting anxiety and my fear of dying.

"Geralyn, you're not scared of dying, you're scared of living."

She explains that since my life now has such a possible ending, it is a wake-up call that I am mortal, which most people are able to deny. Most people stay in jobs they hate, marriages that are miserable, and just postpone joy because they think they have so much time left to figure it all out. Honey's advice does not make sense at first, but she is very smart and spiritual and when I start to think about it more I do start to realize that the potential of life is freaking me out. If this is all there is, my one shot, I need to get it all in *fast*. No waiting.

I make a list of everything I want to do. But I get scared that the list is not significant enough. There is not enough gravitas on it. I mean, I never wanted to skydive or climb Mount Everest. Should I quit my job, leave my husband, travel the world, now that I might die? How do I live up to this drama?

I decide that maybe the most courageous thing I can do is to try to return to my regular life, with the knowledge that there is nothing regular about it. And returning to my marriage seems like my biggest challenge. I remember Tyler crying when I was first diagnosed and saying that he was scared I might leave him and how crazy it sounded then. I had been thinking *he* might leave. But now I understand what he meant. Since everything has changed, how could we remain the same? Tyler has been there for me in his own way. He just bought me an amazing black satin suit with zippers that he told me matched my new haircut, and he was right. But he still hasn't come with me to my check-ups to hold my hand.

I could never have imagined the moment when I understood how hard this had been on Tyler. We are in the emergency room, in the same hospital where I had just had my breasts operated on for the last time only weeks ago. My breasts are still tender from the implant surgery. My scar is still raw and bright red. But I am not the patient—Tyler is.

I had found him covered in blood on our bathroom floor. He had slipped on the tiles and gashed his forehead on the corner of the sink. I knew he was drinking when he came home at 2 A.M. and did not want to wake me up by turning on the bathroom light. I had been worried about him. He had felt so distant lately and I understood why he might need to have a drink to temporarily escape the reality that his wife was being treated for breast cancer in the same hospital where he worked. When I heard the slip and the scream I ran in. I turned on the light. The black-and-white tiles were covered in red. Blood was everywhere.

I told Tyler we needed to go to the hospital. He was the doctor, but I knew his head was bleeding too much. He refused.

"Tyler, I'm calling the hospital. This is ridiculous. You're bleeding too much."

He had bled through two of our towels and I was scared he might pass out from shock. I couldn't believe he actually thought he was okay. It was the same denial he used on me.

But all I feel is pity when he is finally lying on the gurney in the ER. A few of his friends have come over to say hi and see why we are here in the middle of the night. I have become quite a regular at Mount Sinai, and Tyler works here round the clock, but strangely now Tyler is the patient. It must be especially humiliating for him because he works here. But there are some perks: They call Tyler's favorite plastic surgeon to stitch up his forehead.

I am staring at Tyler's forehead and the needle going in and out of his skin. As the plastic surgeon is making his stitches I feel so bad for Tyler, and for myself. It feels as if our marriage has been split in half, like Tyler's forehead, like my breast. Like we have been cut open and we are bleeding and the stitches are trying to hold together what has come apart. Will our relationship ever be the same?

I grab Tyler's hand and try to comfort him, but I feel so inadequate. I realize that I can't take away his pain and the stitches and I can't stop the bleeding. Now I know how Tyler must have felt, watching me in the hospital during all my pain. It must have been even worse for him because he is a doctor and he was helpless. He couldn't stop the cancer, the pain, the worry. Maybe being on the sidelines is even more painful than getting the needles, the chemo, the surgery? Whenever I complained to my mom that Tyler was not being supportive, she defended him.

"Geralyn, you haven't seen Tyler's face when you're in surgery. You're not being fair. I've sat with him during those long hours. He's very worried."

Now I can see all of the worry in Tyler's face. The plastic surgeon is finishing the stitches and he tells Tyler he'll definitely have a scar there. No matter how good a job he does tonight.

I think about my mastectomy scar, the long red line hidden safely under my shirt. Tyler's scar is a red line straight down the middle of his forehead for everyone to see: It is so visible. I feel so guilty that I have made everyone in my life go through hell. Maybe Tyler always insisting that I was cured was a huge vote of confidence? Maybe it was helpful. Because seeing him so scared and vulnerable now is making me scared.

It is so strange that we both have fresh red scars. We have both been so scarred by this experience. Tyler has been so reluctant to admit his pain and fear but it feels like now he is finally wearing it on his face, as I had wished he would all along.

13

I'm a Survivor

It is my twenty-ninth birthday. One year ago I was bracing for my mastectomy surgery, so tonight I need to prove that I am back. Watch out.

I am wearing black hot pants and a tight white shirt. I have not worn a white shirt in so long because I was scared it would show my red scar or single nipple. I am wearing my black miracle bra under the white shirt to cover up the flaws, but when I look in the mirror it looks deliberate. I have added some hair products to my buzz cut to make it, too, look deliberate, trying to spike the front few pieces up. I am an inadvertent fashion statement. I had to make my eyeliner darker to make it match the hair.

I am wearing the patent leather high heels that I bought for my chemo treatments. Instead of hearing them click against the white floors of my chemo office, tonight I will hear them click against the polished wood of a very cool club.

I could almost pass as normal—almost, because my right eyebrow has grown back slightly crooked from the chemo. And my veins are now light brown instead of black. I will keep my sleeves down tonight.

I still can't believe that only a year has passed and that so much has changed. I've lost my breast and my hair and my energy and I have gone through four boob blow-ups, four boob surgeries, twelve chemo sessions, and a lot of mental mix-up. When I turned twenty-eight a year ago I was preparing for my mastectomy, but now I'm preparing for a blowout I'm-back-and-if-you-even-doubted-it-for-a-moment-here-I-am party. There is one hesitation. What do I write on my birthday cake? Just celebrating twenty-nine feels trite. In my heart I will always be twenty-eight. My life started and ended on that birthday. I decide that I will be twenty-eight plus one . . . and I tell the bakery they need to squeeze that on the cake in hot pink icing and I don't care if there is an extra icing charge.

Reluctantly, I have started telling people that I am a breast cancer "survivor." It is so different from saying, "I have breast cancer." But am I really a survivor? Suppose that I don't survive? Everyone keeps telling me that I "beat" cancer but I know that it is out of my hands. Will I let my family and friends down if I die? All I want to do is hit thirty.

I need to practice being a survivor. I get the chance when two amazing women, Donna and Porter, invite me to join their "2 Chicks, 2 Bikes, 1 Cause" project. It's my big chance to come out as a survivor. They are riding their bikes across the country to educate young women about breast cancer. My cousin, Mira, tells them about me, and I agree to fly out to their kick-off event in Seattle.

When Rena first reached out to me when I was diagnosed, she made me promise her that I would be there for other women who had just been diagnosed the way that she was there for me. She was a stranger to me when she first called, but her voice gave me so much hope. It was my lifeline. I know that I need to start telling the story of finding my lump when I was only twenty-seven. Maybe the only way to make sense of what has happened to me is to save some other woman's life?

It is my first talk as a "survivor." I am so excited to speak at this event because Julie, the young woman hosting it, has had a recurrence, and I need to meet her. I have been terrified that my cancer might come back, so meeting her feels like such a vote of confidence in my future. That maybe I could face having cancer again. My doctors warn me that I am at a very high risk to recur because I am so young. This chance to meet someone going through a recurrence might reassure me that I can endure that, too.

When I arrive in Seattle, I can't find Julie anywhere. I know she is planning on introducing me when the program starts because we have e-mailed each other. Everyone takes their seats in the auditorium. But instead of Julie there is a doctor at the podium. She begins to talk about what an amazing job Julie did with the event that night, and then, "Julie died today at 5:40."

There is a large gasp in the room.

"Now Geralyn Lucas will speak to us."

I begin to walk but I do not even feel my feet moving or know where I am going. I am heading towards the podium. I need to speak to the audience, I am supposed to inspire them, but now I am only convinced that I am going to die. How can I even call myself a survivor?

Every step forward there is something pulling me towards the podium, and when I get to the front of the audience and stand at the podium I know she is there. Julie. She is passing a torch. I know that I need to save a life. Julie is telling me that I have to. It is the only way we can understand what has happened to her, what has happened to me. Even though I won the seventh-grade public speaking contest, there is nothing that I can say that will sound clever or inspiring. I step up to the microphone but I keep my head down.

"My name is Geralyn Lucas. I just turned twenty-nine. Julie was only thirty-four. We are too young to die."

I cry through my speech, but I end by making them laugh about the one-balled cab driver.

I decide to do the breast cancer walk, for Julie. I write her name on a form they are handing out which says, "I walk in memory of . . ." and pin it on my back. I grab another piece of paper—"I walk in celebration of"—and I write "Rena, Jane, and Meredith." I pick up a pink hat and pink pom-pom socks to wear, which means that I am a "survivor." Maybe being in a crowd of survivors will make me feel more alive or more convinced? But all that I can see is a sea of pink signs that say "In memory of" and list the names of all the women who have died from breast cancer.

Every step of the walk I am trailed by a ghost. Why am I alive and Julie is dead? After all of the pain and suffering those women went through, they deserved to live. Will I live?

I finish the walk and head to a coffee shop. My head is spinning from seeing all the names of women who died of breast cancer. Maybe I am too new a survivor to handle this. I can't be a survivor, not yet. Just as I'm about to take off my pink survivor hat a young woman holding a baby walks up to me.

"Excuse me. Are you a survivor?" She must have seen my pink hat.

I pause for so long that she asks me again, and I nod.

"I came to the walk today to meet a young woman and show her my baby. All my doctors told me not to get pregnant, but I did anyway. I wanted to show my baby to someone to give her some hope."

She doesn't know how badly I need some hope right now. How much I need to believe that I, too, will be a survivor. She lets me hold her baby girl, Maya.

"Weren't you scared to get pregnant because your doctors said not to?"

Her fear and her defiance make me understand the word *survivor* a little bit better. That being a survivor is not all about being feeling feisty and so sure of it. I tell her about Julie's death. How I think that Julie is a survivor, too, even though she died.

Maybe it is not really about if I win or lose against cancer, it is how I played the game. I know now that I am a survivor. Because I have survived the vomiting, the stretching, the uncertainty.

But right about when I start to believe that I'm a survivor, I am robbed again. My Grandma Katie's diamond ring is stolen from my apartment just as everything in my life is returning to "normal." I cry so hard when I discover the ring is stolen. I can never replace that ring, it is too sentimental. I can never get it back. I look for that ring everywhere. It was inscribed, "To Katie, Love Phil." My parents gave me the ring when I was diagnosed as a symbol that my grandma's spirit was with me.

Looking so hard for that ring makes me realize that I think that I have been looking for her everywhere, too: the pre-cancer Geralyn. My breast, my hair, everything that cancer has stolen from me?

What else could I possibly have taken away from me? What is left to rob me of? The one-boobed, bald, broken, tired, depressed woman who used to light up a room and flirt with cab drivers even the day before her mastectomy? What else could I possibly have to be stolen? I had lost so much in the brief nine months of hell it just frightened and overwhelmed me. Actually, *loss* is too banal a word to describe what I was feeling about the cancer. I had been robbed. Robbed of my innocence about life and my health and my future, robbed of an actual piece of me. Why was I robbed *again*?

I have a strange dream. I had found everything that I had ever lost. I am not talking about the one sock that disappears in the dryer. I mean the things that were stolen.

My boyfriend, Flip, who Karen stole from me at my high school prom after I passed out from too much champagne,

My German Shepherd, Tippy, who I spent my entire childhood with, who had to be put to sleep right before I went off to college,

My long black hair that had fallen out during my chemo,

There were a lot of things . . . and when they started swirling and mingling together I realized they were all irreplaceable. No other ring would be my grandmother's, no wig could equal my own hair, and I couldn't go out and buy a brand new breast. There was a unifying theme in all of the objects, too. No matter how hard I had looked, they were lost forever. At least with a needle in a haystack, there is a needle that you know is there. These things were gone.

When I woke up, first there was the disappointment that it was just a dream. And then it occurred to me. Yes, the ring was gone—but Grandma Katie wasn't. No one could steal her from me—ever. Maybe, when I was facing the largest loss of my life, she had arranged for the ring to disappear?

She could never be stolen from me. I never believed in life after death, but I now believe that Grandma Katie is trying to reach out to me through the robbery. She is showing me that her memory is too fierce to get stolen with the ring, that she is there in my heart. Maybe she is showing me that even though so much has been stolen from me, I am still here. I still exist despite all the losses.

I thought that diamonds are supposed to be forever. I am not so sure of forevers now. Nothing feels certain.

But I am a survivor.

I survived this hell.

I decide I will steal it all back.

14

My Monet

I begin to procrastinate about the nipple. Because the reconstruction took so long, hurt so much, and went over budget, I thought I would be eager to get my finishing touch: the nipple. Maybe it's like finally hanging up the drapes or applying the last coat of varnish on your newly installed hardwood floors.

My plastic surgeon, Dr. P, sensing my nipple nervousness, is trying to get me to schedule the procedure when I am at an appointment in her office. She has the photo book out and she opens it up. She has built me the perfect boob and I know that if anyone can make a perfect nipple, it is Dr. P. I did not realize just how seriously she takes her nipples.

"I make a Seurat nipple."

My mom is with me and it catches us both off guard.

"Most plastic surgeons tattoo the new nipple skin only one color with the tattoo ink. But an areola"—she is calling a nipple by its medical name—"is not one color. They have different shades. When the light hits a nipple there are different colors."

I look down at my nipple and she is right—it is a masterpiece of creamy pinks and whites and maroon and definitely not one shade. My mom and I are enraptured as she continues.

"I make pointillist nipples. Different shades with dots of color. I make the best nipple in the world. Really, it's hard to tell which one is real and which is the nipple I've painted."

I am suddenly so relieved that I was required to take an art history course as an undergraduate because now I finally understand beauty and art, and the universe might make sense. I am seeing Monet's waterlilies. I am picturing his beautiful strokes that blend and somehow move together to create a gorgeous hue that seems so real. Waterlilies are seducing me. The thought of a museum-quality nipple is comforting. When I look up at Dr. P and her photos of nipples I see she is wearing an antique gold, jewel-encrusted sword on the lapel of her white doctor coat. Family heirlooms do inspire confidence at a time like this. I remember her in the operating room in her blue scrubs, her blue face mask, her hair net, and her beautiful blue eyes. She was wearing a gorgeous strand of pearls around her neck. She has taste and class. She will complete me.

As a finishing touch, Dr. P explains the importance of light in her work. A perfect nipple should not be created under fluorescent light because, hopefully, my nipple will not be viewed in such harsh lighting. She will bring me to the window while tattooing to get the color right in natural light. This was the best sales job I had ever heard.

And I am craving a nipple because suddenly nipples are "in," a must-have accessory. Thin, sheer white shirts worn without bras are the rage. I miss my nipple. I miss the freedom of not wearing a bra, of wearing a thin T-shirt and seeing the outline of my nipples underneath. I miss my symmetry and I miss bikini tops and tank tops and I especially missed my nipple when Tyler took me to St. Lucia to celebrate my last reconstruction surgery and I inadvertently ended up on a topless beach. All of the European tourists were sunbathing topless and I didn't have the courage to take off my bathing suit top. It would have involved too much explaining and I was tired.

When I share my nipple ambivalence with my mom, she is not buying it. She is positive that it will make me feel complete and calls constantly to nipple-nag. She even leaves me a desperate message from a cell phone saying she is sitting next to a woman on the Metroliner on her way home to Philadelphia, they got to talking, and the woman told her she had just finished her breast cancer treatments and had just gotten her nipple done. My mom tells me it looks fabulous, and the woman is screaming into the phone in the background that she loves her nipple—no one can tell which one is real, blah, blah.

I schedule my nipple surgery but I begin wavering about getting my new nipple. I am confident about Dr. P's nipple aptitude, but a strange thought pops into my head that I can't stop: Who would I be fooling? I would know that it was a fake. Tyler would definitely know it was counterfeit. Would it be for the people at the topless beach? In a Loehmann's communal dressing room? For prancing around the gym locker room? Is my nipple about blending? About being an imposter? About pretending I still have a boob when I really don't? It suddenly feels so, well, inauthentic. Grandma Katie's ring being stolen helped me understand that my nipple was gone and there was just no replacing it.

The day of my scheduled nipple surgery I am instead standing on a grungy street corner in the East Village trying to work up courage to go inside the tattoo parlor.

I want to put my own signature on my mound and I want something meaningful. This is not Monet, but it is art. This will be my Monet.

I am on my own and really miss Dr. P's pearls when I see the dirty steps leading up to the parlor. I know Grandma Katie is pushing me to walk up the steps. I had no idea what to wear to a tattoo parlor, but I knew I had to look cool. I chose dark sunglasses and all black, except for the red heart on my T-shirt. My heart is going to guide me to the tattoo parlor. If my mind chickens out, my heart will make me stay. I am so sick of wearing my heart on my sleeve that I have decided I need it permanently etched on my boob instead. I need to remember my mojo.

I know I don't look like I belong in a tattoo parlor even though I have bought a satin leopard-print push-up bra just to fit in. Wearing the leopard bra feels racy. I feel the satin sliding between my shirt and my skin and I realize that it is the first time I have actually felt something other than a needle on that breast. The fabric is so soft. I have tried to feel my husband's hands on that breast, but I couldn't really feel much of anything but pain.

I need to walk around the block, and strange images of myself keep flashing through my head. I still think of myself as the goody girl, the preppie, the high school newspaper editor, and the prude. Can I pull this off?

I need to show what I feel inside. I need to tell my story of fear and the courage that came from it.

When I floated the idea of getting a real tattoo instead of a nipple tattoo my parents told me that I could never be buried in a Jewish cemetery because Jewish law prohibited desecrating one's body. So I enlisted my Grandmother Ruth's husband, Irving, the most religious member in our family, for a fact check. He left me a message on my answering machine three days later.

"Geralyn. This is Irving. I met a rabbi named Shmuel. He has three tattoos." Coast was clear.

I pulled every Internet article I could find about tattoo artists and began to call around New York City. Every man who answered the phone sounded gruff, like he was covered with very scary tattoos—daggers or swastikas.

"Joe's Tattoo Parlor."

(I was feeling shy, but I knew that I was going from the kiddie pool to the deep end and there was no changing my mind now.)

"Can you do a tattoo on a breast reconstruction after a mastectomy? Will the implant burst?"

I was obsessed with my implant bursting—exploding—in a tattoo parlor. It would be a very dramatic scene. My chest would just collapse, and someone would scream, *Call the paramedics! Her implant burst!* I would be taken away in an ambulance (would they turn on the siren and run a red light for a burst implant?) and when I arrived in the emergency room there would be whispering among the hospital staff that there was a burst implant in the house, picked up at a tattoo parlor. Medical students in the hospital might line up to see my deflated boob and I might end up as a

case history photo in a medical textbook. Either that or as an ur-
ban legend.

And I imagined being back in Dr. P's pristine Park Avenue office and having to explain to her the trouble I had caused. She
would be in her scrubs with her pearl necklace, her forgiving but
rolling eyes looking at me like I was her crazy teenage daughter
who had done something very naughty.

I was terrified of what would actually happen if my implant
burst. Would my chest be flat and really show me there was nothing between that implant and me? That implant was blown up
with some sort of hope, and maybe I was a little terrified that the
tattoo needle might burst that layer of hope. The thought of getting expanded again in Dr. P's office was almost enough to make
me change my plan. Strrrrretching, pulling, yanking at my skin
again was too much to think about.

Until Joshua answered the phone. His voice sounded so sweet
and reassuring that I thought that I had misdialed and gotten a
New Age spa or a therapist's office.

"Tattoo Heaven, Josh speaking."

I heard buzzing in the background and I knew that I had
reached a real tattoo parlor.

"Hi." My voice sounded way too high and sweet to be calling a
tattoo parlor. I tried to deepen it a little for my next sentence. "I
was wondering if you could do a tattoo on a breast reconstruction
after a mastectomy? Will the implant burst?"

I was waiting to see if he thought this was a crank call and if he
might start cracking up on the other end of the line, but he seemed
very knowledgeable, and serious.

"There are ten layers of skin until your implant and I would
only need to go three deep."

I suddenly felt like we were having a quasi-medical conversation. I felt so relieved and thought that Dr. P might even approve of my finding such a knowledgeable and competent tattoo artist. Then he added the most important piece of information.

"My grandmother died of breast cancer. I want to donate my time to do your tattoo. I've never done an implant before. But I've done women who were not reconstructed. I've done beautiful oceans and rainbows on their mastectomy scars."

"Josh, I'm so scared. I've never been to a tattoo parlor. I am really embarrassed to ask, but do you use clean needles?"

It sort of felt like a safe-sex conversation, but I knew we needed to talk about safe needles. I already had cancer, I had just finished chemo, and I did not want hepatitis C. When Josh assured me that he used clean needles there were no more excuses. I scheduled my tattoo appointment for today.

But now, standing on the grimy steps, I am scared. Josh sees me outside and comes to get me. In person, he is as beautiful as he sounded. His eyes are green and soulful, and he is so gentle, except for the bad-ass thunderbolt tattooed on his neck. I am trying to be cool but I am really worried that I have left Dr. P's museum world. If she was an impressionist, Joshua is, at best, a graffiti artist. There are bold, shocking images covering the wall. The floors are grainy, it looks like sawdust has been sprinkled on them, and there is a faint buzzing coming from the back room—the sound of a needle burning dye into flesh.

Now I am scared because tattoos are permanent. What if I don't like it? It will be there forever. But I sort of like the idea of it on my body, especially if I do die of cancer. Maybe it will make the undertaker smirk? Maybe, when I am being prepared for burial, they will see I was a fighter, that I was a feisty one who did not go gentle into that good night?

Josh must see my reluctance and decides now is the time to review his rules with me. Well, actually, it was just one big rule. No guy's name on my boob. He personally knew that Johnny Depp had to change his *Winona Forever* tattoo to *Wino Forever*, and still seemed slightly traumatized by the experience.

I already know exactly what I want for my tattoo and after I explain it, Josh spends two hours sketching the tattoo design. I want a heart. Not the kind of poofy heart you draw in high school—I want a serious heart to remind me how courageous it is to follow my heart. I want wings on the top to represent all the angels who showed me that I would get my life back: the one-balled cab driver; the stripper who was giving it away but still swaggered; the nurse who helped me wipe myself when I was trying to be glamorous and not use a bedpan; my Amazons: Meredith, Rena, and Jane.

The placement of the tattoo is key. I tell Josh that I want it right at the lower end of my scar, much lower than a nipple would be. It is not replacing the nipple and I do not want it to be perfectly centered. I want the heart to look like it's flying up, soaring away. Where my scar ends, my courage and hope begin. The heart should be outlined in black but inside will be the shade of the bright red lipstick I wore to my surgery. In the right corner of the heart, there will be the two wings outlined in black. Josh thinks we should shade them in with white, but I like seeing only my skin through the wings.

When I take my satin leopard bra off and stand in front of Josh, I know that my mound really is a breast because of the way he is looking at it. At me. This is the first time a man has seen the mound, the first time that I am topless in front of another man except for my husband (and my breast surgeon, but he doesn't count). I cannot believe how hard Josh looks. When I look at him just looking at me, I start to apologize for how awkward this must be for him to have to see me like this. There is a sort of an unspoken conversation where Josh tells me that he still thinks I am hot without my boob and that he really can't help but take a long look. I am shocked, and just to prove I am not imagining his interest he looks me straight in the eyes: "Geralyn. You are a very foxy woman."

As he starts the tattooing, the pain on my breast reminds me of all the pain I have been through: the drains, the stitches, the bandages, the stretching—and I black out. Josh gets me Oreos and we continue. I am not leaving with half a tattoo. As the pain continues, I feel a sudden burst of euphoria; Josh says that my natural endorphins are kicking in to combat the pain. But I know that this is what courage must feel like.

When he leads me to the mirror to look at myself I feel the same fear as when Dr. B removed my bandage in the hospital. I am scared to look and start thinking I have made a huge mistake.

I close my eyes and slowly take a peep. The mirror is playing a trick on me. When I first see the red of the heart, I think—for a flash—it is my nipple, and for a flash I see my old breast. I hold the mirror so that I will see just my new breast—it is still too painful to compare it to my other one.

I think about Monet's waterlilies and remember my old nipple and something about this one is so bold that it forces my eyes to focus and I look and look and look until I think I see what is there. There are no waterlilies. No soft hues. No dancing and blending color.

Va-va-voom! It is red. And bold. And powerful! A karmic

boomerang hits me and everything that was robbed from me, my breast, my nipple, my hope, my innocence, my beauty, returns for that moment and then some. Because so much has been taken from me, that much more is now here, almost screaming its existence at me.

I see that I am sort of pieced back together. I think maybe I have found my new right breast right here in this tattoo parlor in the East Village. I am finally able to say good-bye to my real right breast, which I still hope is in a Tupperware container in a pathology refrigerator as my husband had promised.

I was *born* into a certain body, but I have *become* this one, I have fashioned part of it and I feel powerful. This is the breast I have chosen. It is not hiding its battle scar—it is wearing it proudly. This is its story.

I go back to work at *20/20* after I get my tattoo. I show several colleagues—it is bad judgment but I am delirious. In order to show my tattoo (which is not in the center of my boob, but in the corner, at the end of my diagonal mastectomy scar), I need to pull my shirt and bra all the way down and it shows my whole new boob. I don't think of it as a boob—to me it's just an expander implant mound, but the looks I am getting make me realize it is more.

When I come home, there are a dozen red roses from Tyler as a vote of confidence for the tattoo. I make sure he closes his eyes and that I have the wings positioned so they are jutting out of my leopard bra before he takes a look. I want him to love it, and he does! It is not a nipple, but it does excite him.

I am so pleased with my tattoo that I become something of an exhibitionist. It's ironic considering how scared I was initially about anyone ever seeing how different I really looked. I show my doorman, and I even show the Amtrak conductor who has a letter of his name on each knuckle: S-A-L-L-Y. Each time I show the tattoo I pull my shirt and bra down. Each time I am learning that my implant mound has become sort of a breast, at least to other people. I like that my tattoo makes people smile instead of the scared faces I am used to seeing when people see my scar and that I was missing a nipple. The tattoo makes me laugh and is now my constant reminder in case I ever forget.

It is so important to follow my heart.

15

Vomit

I want a baby. I am back in the same hospital, having my blood drawn. But in this blood test they will look for signs of a baby, not like my routine blood tests that look for signs of a tumor and the blood tests from my chemo that measured my white counts. I hate the way the needle feels in my vein. It is too familiar.

I have been vomiting again, constantly, and I think I might be pregnant. Even though it might be a baby that is making me vomit, the vomit tastes like my chemo vomit.

I was told that I needed to wait at least two years before I could even think of getting pregnant, to see if my cancer would come back. It has been four. And I was told that pregnancy was dangerous and could make my cancer come back even if it hadn't already, because my hormones would be hundreds of times my normal levels. The doctors are worried that any small cancer cells floating around could go wild with those hormones. My mom and my sister-in-law Wendy offered to be my surrogate. They must love me a lot to be willing to vomit for me.

The waiting has been excruciating. I was unsure if my body could have a baby and if I could, was it even fair to have a child if I might die? And what about my eggs going through all that poisoning? Were they still normal? I did research. I found studies about women who went through chemo and then had babies. Their eggs seemed okay. I read the fine print—the profiles of the subjects. I got the entire way to the bottom of the scientific paper, and on the bottom of the page was print so small that I had to squint: Subject 34 had seven children after her breast cancer treatment. Seven! Was it a typo? Seven! Silly number seven made me believe during all my tests to see if my cancer had come back before I got pregnant. I sang sevens in the bone scan, when I was told to hold my breath with the heavy lead apron on during my chest x-ray, and I swear I could make out the number seven on the sonogram screen during my liver profile.

And then I met Erin. She was assigned to me as a story at my job at *20/20*. She was a young mother dying of cancer and she had a toddler daughter, Peyton. Erin decided to videotape certain lessons for Peyton to watch after Erin had died. The man who gave me the assignment was not Mr. Sensitive, he was very matter of fact.

"Geralyn, call this woman. She's dying of breast cancer and making videotapes for her young daughter so the girl won't forget her. Here's her phone number. Sounds like a good story, right?"

Meredith was horrified when she realized that he'd given me this project. She made him call me back to express some fake concern.

"If this is too hard for you to work on, then we'll reassign it."

But it was too late. I had already called Erin. And I wanted to hear her story.

She and her husband, Doug, were reluctant to share their story with anyone because they were wary that their story would become too tabloid. I understood their fear, and in an attempt to offer some credibility I explained that I had just had breast cancer. Instead of being reassured, she surprised me with her hesitation.

"Will this story be too hard for you to work on, Geralyn? I'm going to die."

I couldn't believe she was thinking about me with everything she was facing. I told her that maybe her story would lead me to some answers I had been searching for.

"Erin, I think about this all the time. I'm so scared. Please tell your story for me and all the other women who need this hope."

She explained that the hardest part was starting the video camera. On the first tape she had started and stopped five times. She kept crying, then saying, "Pardon," and turning off the camera. I think it was the hardest part because she knew that in that beginning was her end. That when her daughter saw that tape, she would no longer be there to hold her. After that, Erin became a madwoman, recording through the night. The video camera was her new umbilical cord to her daughter. It was her salvation.

Erin's courage answered my greatest fear about leaving a child motherless. Erin would always be Peyton's mom, and she had found a way to stay in Peyton's life.

But it was not that easy to grasp. Just when I had worked up my confidence to try to get pregnant, I saw the little girl holding the pink stuffed bunny rabbit in my oncologist's office. God must have placed her there to taunt me. The first thing I noticed, which anyone would have noticed, was that the velvety fur was missing from the bunny—it had almost bald patches. And the next thing I noticed was the little girl gripping her bunny, holding onto the fur that was left. She was standing next to a seat in the waiting room. Then her mom walked out and that's when it made sense: Her mom's hair had fallen out, in patches, like the bunny's. Her mom had breast cancer. I was at an after-chemo check-up. I had come to see my oncologist, Dr. O, to ask her permission to get pregnant. Erin had showed me a way. But the pink bunny was not a vote of confidence. My mom had come with me for support. She saw the pink bunny, too. We both started to cry.

I kept focused on my goal. I wanted Dr. O's approval. There were magical reasons to get pregnant: To trust my body again. To believe in the future again. To run towards life and away from death. To pick up where Tyler and I left off before my diagnosis. Tyler told me he wanted me to have a baby so that he could always be with me. He wanted to take a piece of me into the world with him in case I died. He promised he would always be there for her, that he could handle being a single dad.

I didn't get Dr. O's approval. Not even close. She lowered her eyes and almost whispered, "It is so hard to take care of sick mothers. It is so sad." I was about to challenge her until I remembered the pink bunny that I had just seen in the waiting room, and I knew that she had seen things that would ruin any joy in motherhood.

But I needed to have a baby. I had earned this. I was a sherpa who had scaled Mount Everest with the fragile eggs in my backpack. Every step over the jagged and steep terrain, I watched my breath in front of me, but I worried more about the hope trailing behind me. Every time I stumbled, I only wanted to protect the eggs. But now that I had finished my trek, with my eggs not broken, I realized I had maybe a bigger trek ahead.

My body was there, my eggs were okay, but my mind was unsteady. Was it irresponsible to have a baby if I could die on it? What kind of mother would that make me? If I did manage to have a normal baby, and beat all the odds, there was still the greatest problem: I might die. The baby might never remember me. Suppose I had a daughter. Would she live her life under a cloud of fear because of her own breasts? Would she resent my cancerous breast and see it as a road map of her own doomed destiny?

When I heard that Erin had died, I was sad and scared. But her death strangely convinced me that I, too, should become a mom. I was haunted by how unfair it was that she was robbed from Peyton, but I loved how she tricked the cancer and found a way to be Peyton's mom forever. Erin gave me my baby.

When I miss my period, I think it might be menopause. At the hospital, they tell me that I need a blood test and sonogram, just like the sonogram that saw my cancer for the first time. This sonogram will show clump of cells, too, but not like the cancer.

It is a baby.

I get genetic testing to see if the baby is okay after all the poison my eggs endured. I should be relieved when the genetics counselor calls me.

"Congratulations, you're having a healthy baby girl."

But all I can think about are her breasts and her future. Will she live under a cancer cloud? Fear of death circles me like a vulture. I become obsessed that my child will be motherless. It sends me into a depression. I do research and find a group called "Motherless Daughters." Rosie O'Donnell's mother and Madonna's mother died when they were young, from breast cancer—Rosie and Madonna turned out normal, right?

When I begin to vomit from morning sickness, I remember the vomiting from chemo. It reminds me that even when I am about to embark on creating a new life, there is unfinished business lurking. Vomiting becomes my bridge between death and life . . . the connection between the oncology office and the maternity ward. Although I had mastered vomiting systems, nothing prepared me for leaving the cancer ward and entering the maternity ward: I went from a world of death to a world of life.

Vomiting is a constant reminder that for me these two worlds are connected, and I can never just leave one for the other.

When they put the microphone to my stomach to try to hear the baby's heartbeat, I swear it is so loud that I imagine it is reverberating all the way to the cancer ward. It is so loud that maybe the IV poles are stirring in the chemo room. Maybe they have all heard its hope? It is pulsating and screaming that a life has gone on. I imagine her heartbeat ricocheting through the white sterile hallways: "life, life, life" is what I hear each time the machine beeps.

But I feel like an imposter in both worlds: I am embarrassed to be pregnant in the cancer ward. It feels like I am betraying my comrades. As they remain in the land of the dead, I have moved on to life. In the maternity ward, I think about them. I cannot believe we are in one hospital, only floors apart.

I am so scared when my body starts to grow during the pregnancy. How can I trust it is growing a baby and not a tumor? How will my body know what to do when it has gone haywire before?

I remain obsessed with the idea of dying on my daughter. I think often of Erin and Peyton, and my biggest fear is that I will die before my daughter has time to remember me. Tyler will be there for her, but a father is not the same as a mother.

I still go to work every day and I am vomiting again constantly. I am now in maternity clothing and my real boob is starting to grow again, on the left side, so now I have begun wearing my other falsie again to even myself out—but I switched to the right side. I am so glad that I threw out only one and kept the other. My stomach is expanding, and I cannot believe all the different variations of myself that have existed in this one office. What do my colleagues think when they see me in the elevator? What else can enlarge itself on my body?

It is hard to keep up the new downtown look in maternity clothes, but I try. I wear everything in black and even find a pair of leopard platforms that I can squeeze my pregnant feet into.

Every time I am at Dr. O's office, I search for the pink bunny and the little girl and her balding mom. I wonder about them. I wonder about us—me and my baby—and I wonder if we will be back in oncology together. I cannot bear to be so pregnant in the oncology ward. I know that everyone is looking at me and remembering how I was one of them, and now I have left them. But I want to tell them that I am really here with them in this world of cancer and death. I just cannot leave it.

This is where I belong.

16

Leo, Not Cancer

When I walk into my baby shower the first thing I notice is all the pink—and I panic. Pink is precarious and dangerous to me now: I have been wearing pink ribbons since my diagnosis.

Everyone knows that I am having a little girl. The pink at the shower is reminding me of the pink signs from breast cancer walks and runs—signs that say "In memory of" for all the lives stolen by breast cancer.

My friend Jen, and her mom Jane, who has survived breast cancer, are insistent that they throw me my baby shower. Jane's toast reminds us all that this is not an average baby shower: "This is a very special baby shower."

Before I open my presents, I lose it.

"I feel uncomfortable opening presents," I start to sob. "You've already given me this baby. Because I know if anything were to happen to me, I know you will all fill in for me."

I decide that I will explain my ordeal to my daughter in her name. I will name her "Skye" because my hypnotherapist had told me that any time I felt any pain I should think of myself as like the sky, because of its resilience. Whatever happens to the sky—a thunderstorm, paint being thrown at it, an airplane flying across it—it is still the sky and remains unchanged. Every needle, every surgery, I said, "I am like the sky." I decide to add an "e" to make it more legitimate. Her middle name will be Meredith for my boss Meredith, and just in case she is a Republican and "Skye" is too out there for her. Meredith has never had a baby because of her health, and I remember how scared I was to tell her that I was pregnant. I was scared because she never got to do this. "Meredith, I feel so strange telling you I'm pregnant. I feel guilty because this is something you couldn't do."

"But Geralyn, I'm so happy for you."

And I know she is. Meredith gives me hair ribbons for my daughter. They were hers when she was a little girl—she had always hoped her daughter could wear them. Now Skye Meredith will.

Skye's name feels like a perfect way to explain our journey together and to look towards her future. Maybe it also shows all the changes I've gone through and still managed to cling to myself. Maybe it's a hope that if Skye's life is filled with clouds and storms there can still be a pink sunset. Maybe after rain and thunder a rainbow will somehow appear.

Robin made me a quilt that has a picture on it of us with

our arms around each other when we were six years old. The picture is surrounded by a sky with beautiful clouds in honor of the name Skye. Robin's present reminds me of her support in my life—always. I know she will always be a part of Skye's life, too.

That night, the phone rings at 11 P.M. It is my younger brother Howard.

"Geralyn, Grandma Ruth died tonight."

He is crying and his voice sounds so small and he is trying to explain that our grandmother fell out of her bed at the nursing home. She was eighty-five and had lived a full life. But I feel as if I have been robbed again.

As I stand in the cemetery at her grave with my family around me, my feet sink into the warm earth and it does not make any sense to me. I am so pregnant that my largest black maternity dress can't even be zipped at the top—it's held together with safety pins. Why would my grandmother be denied this chance to meet her great-granddaughter by only days?

The rabbi tries to assure me that they have met: two souls, one on the way up and one on the way down. She is very convincing, but I am not buying any of it. This is another robbery when I am feeling so vulnerable.

A religious man pulls me aside and tells me that it is very bad luck to be in a cemetery when pregnant.

"It's bad luck that my grandmother died right before her great-granddaughter was born," I snap back. Life is not making any sense lately.

I have not been in a cemetery since I was diagnosed with cancer. I have not seen a body lowered into the earth and felt the reality so strongly. As my grandmother's coffin is lowered into the sloppy hole in the earth I feel myself being tugged down with her.

All around us there are tombstones with women's names, and I start calculating all the ages on the tombstones to figure out if a mother has died young. "Beloved Mother" appears everywhere.

The baby is kicking hard but I feel like I should stay here, with my grandmother, with the dead. I am an imposter in the land of the living, and it is only a matter of time.

My grandmother's sister-in-law tries to comfort me when I start to sob.

"It's so unfair. My grandmother will never know my daughter, Skye. How could this happen?"

"Geralyn, you'll see your grandmother now more than ever in your daughter."

I look at her and realize she must know what she is talking about. At ninety-two, she has seen plenty of funerals.

I start contracting when I leave the cemetery. They have been trying to induce me for over a week. I have been contracting wildly, but not dilating. When my water breaks that night, my doctors tell me that I need to deliver the baby within twenty-four hours to prevent infection.

When I check into the hospital with my parents and Tyler, I do not smell life here, not even a whiff of it. All I smell is the smell of death that has trailed me from my cancer. It smells fake sweet and sanitary, like it has been sprayed and washed to cover up the nasty odor underneath. There is a desperation smell, a bad-news smell, a smell of needles and x-rays, and tumors and blood. I cannot smell a baby.

I start to realize this is not the place to bring a baby into the world. I remember everything I left in that hospital.

I left my right breast, my lymph nodes, my bloody bandages, my half-dead roses.

Now, I am supposed to leave with a baby.

But I am still not dilating enough to let her out. Maybe I think I can keep her and be pregnant forever and that way I can never get cancer again. We are together and I am scared that once I release her she might lose me. I want to stay pregnant and with her. I like being pregnant because the doctors are always checking on the baby—they just assume that I am fine.

I freak out and call my hypnotherapist to tell her that I am in a house of death. That this is no place to start a life. She tells me that the hospital gave me life last time, and it will give me life again.

Skye is so late that she will now be a Leo, not a Cancer. (Her due date was July twenty-second but even after three inductions, she is not coming out.) I know that it is only a horoscope, but I think that maybe this is her first present to me. Maybe she knows my panic about the word *cancer* Cancer had been a tumor to me . . . how could it mean a birthday? Maybe she knows that I am scared I will die on her.

I need a C-section because I am still not dilating. Despite all the contractions, I still cannot let her go. I am holding on to her too tightly.

I know how to prepare for surgery. I put on the hairnet, the hospital gown, the scratchy slippers. I am wheeled into an operating room again. I see the stainless steel. I am cut open again. But they are not removing cancer, they are taking out the baby. I can only see Tyler's eyes above the surgical mask but I can now see Skye's future. I know he will be there for her. Even if I die, Tyler and I have found a way to be together.

When they pull her out of me it is as if I have crossed the finish line. If I died right then and there in that operating room it would not matter. I've tricked my destiny. I've grown cells that were not malignant. I've grown a future. I've grown a smile.

When I hold my baby for the first time I realize that Grandma Ruth is showing me that love lives longer than our bodies can. Maybe her exit was her final gift to me. I obsessed so much about dying during my pregnancy that finding myself in a cemetery brought things into pretty clear focus. Her death answered my deepest secret fear about my daughter. Would she forget me if I died? I know now that my baby will never forget me. I know that my death will compel her to know me, to remember me, as I will remember my grandmother and tell my daughter about her.

In a strange way I felt my grandmother was more with me than I had felt her in a long time. She hadn't vanished.

I always thought that life was supposed to be fair. But it's hard to describe what is fair about my new baby's life starting while my own feels so shaky. I think that my grandmother and Erin have shown me that we can always be together.

Dr. B is the first visitor to hold Skye. Same hospital. Same month that I was diagnosed with cancer, but now five years later and I am Skye's mom.

"Thank you, Dr. B. Thank you for believing I would have this day."

Dr. B had told me on that day five years ago that I would get my life back. I never believed him. I am still unsure. When he picks Skye up and strokes her tiny perfect arm, I see her little wrist with the hospital bracelet. I remember all of my other hospital bracelets.

I can barely stand up on the day I am supposed to check out of the hospital. I am determined to walk home with Skye in my arms, but my doctors are reluctant to let me because of the Cesarean section. The morphine has worn off and the stitches pull and stretch my skin every time I take a step. I have practiced standing up for two minutes at a time. At first my legs felt tingling and I saw black spots. They bring me out in a wheelchair, to the sliding glass doors at the front of the hospital. I stand up and I grip Skye harder. I have never been able to walk home from the hospital. I had always had drains sewn in me; I was always too dizzy from the blood loss to walk. After all my other hospital visits I would always take a taxi home and even that was unbearable for the six short blocks because I felt every bump in that back seat. I was not stitched up tight enough.

I am still dizzy. But I need to prove to myself that I am okay. I am her mom. I can take care of her. She will be safe with me. I promise her that I will not return to that hospital if I can help it. I need to carry her into a new world. Although it is only six blocks home, it feels like a marathon. My marathon. For every step I take I feel a stab of a pain. I grip her harder. As I take each step I remember how delicate life is—like the sleeping newborn in my arms.

I had forgotten why they sold "Congratulations" cards in hospitals.

I had forgotten that somehow, life could follow death.

I had forgotten that sometimes Cancer could be a birthday.

17

The Booby Mafia

It was our first night together. I see through the nursery glass that she is crying and I need to rescue her. I wheel her little plastic cube down the hallway and into my room and I take her out of the plastic wheeler. When I put her on my chest, suddenly, miraculously, she begins breast-feeding on my left breast. The baby is actually getting milk from the nipple. My baby stops crying and I just look down, in awe that I am actually feeding this baby. So this is what boobs were invented for? Not cancer—not chemo, not mastectomies, not implants, not skin stretching. Not strip bars. Just milk!

I think I got my boob back. And my groove back. There is dreamy milk and I breast-feed everywhere I go—I used to be so embarrassed for those women and now I am becoming one. I whip it out in dressing rooms, in restaurant bathrooms—and even in the office with the door closed. I'm not that bold!

One night at 4 A.M. she is crying and I am giving her my boob and feeling so confident that she is voracious, and I can feed her. But when I turn on the TV and start channel surfing, I land at some porn. The men and women are all going for the boobs, too. I look down at Skye in her boob bliss. Why is it all about boobs? Even babies are obsessed. Can I really be her mom with just one? I am trying my hardest.

I saved my left breast with the hope that someday I might nurse a baby. I wanted my breast to feed a baby, not kill me. I agonized over whether I should have a double mastectomy when I was first diagnosed, but I held out hope. I worried that the cancer would return in that breast, and during my exams I would shake and sweat and worry that my other breast had cancer, too.

But I didn't realize that making milk would bring its own set of worries. It will take more than mojo to breast-feed Skye with one boob. She is the biggest girl in the nursery at eight pounds, five ounces and, just like her mom, she loves to eat. My boob seems to be working, but then one day the bonding is over. She will not latch on and only wants a bottle. I call a hospital to speak with a lactation consultant and explain my case: I have one boob but I am breast-feeding. When the consultant hears this, she insists that I come into the hospital. Tyler and my friends and family think that I should just give Skye formula. But I need my boob to work.

The lactation consultant seems determined to make me a one-boobed, breast-feeding pin-up girl the minute I arrive in her office. She informs me that she has good news! She has done some research and there is a cult in China that only believed in nursing children off their right breast—how amazing that there are other one-breasted breast-feeders in the world!

"In fact"—she is now really excited—"one breast will produce as much milk as two because the baby is constantly nursing on it."

But my pediatrician has never heard of such a Chinese cult and tells me that he thinks the breast-feeding militants can be cultlike in their breast-feeding frenzy. He warns me that Skye still needs formula.

But my boob is not producing enough milk and when I start calling other breast-feeding support groups for solutions to my one-boobed dilemma, I begin to notice a pattern. All the breast-feeders seem to have the same agenda and seem like loosely affiliated conspirators. I call them the Booby Mafia. They live by one motto: "Breast Is Best!" Their code of honor demands that breast-feeding is acceptable anywhere, and if you have a problem with that then you definitely were not breast-fed and must be disturbed. After all, who would ever dare come between a suckling infant and its mom? They have different names—La Leche League, the Militant Breast-feeders, lactation consultants—but just one obsession: breast-feeding. And if you challenge their power, watch out. It is especially hard to question their way after being in labor for three days, having a C-section, and feeling weepy.

They have compared notes and their stories match: breast-fed babies have higher IQs; their poops smell better; they are better adjusted; they have fewer ear infections, and lower rates of cancer and obesity; and there has never been a breast-fed serial killer. Okay they don't say that, but they kind of imply it.

The Booby Mafia all speak in terms that I have never heard before and quote extensive literature on the subject. And that is when my lactation consultant uses the first Booby Mafia term: nipple confusion. I think that maybe she is referring to my tattoo—that my daughter might see the bright red heart and confuse it with the one real nipple that I do have. No. Not that type of confusion. It's more scientific. The Booby Mafia explains that I cannot give my daughter a bottle: That would create "nipple confusion" because my daughter would forget how to suck the breast, which requires more work than a bottle nipple. And to add confusion to the nipple confusion, there are different kinds of nipples on bottles and the Booby Mafia was emphatic that the only nipple to use is the Advent bottle from London. The Advent is advertised as mimicking the breast nipple, meaning it actually takes me longer to feed the baby because the baby has to suck harder to get the formula.

My lactation consultant tells me to only use the Advent bottles if I am desperate. Otherwise, I'm supposed to give her formula in a little cup—it looks like a tequila shot glass, actually, especially at midnight. Yes, strangely, an infant even knows how to drink out of a shot glass. It is awkward at first, but it is the key to "supplementation." That is the next Booby Mafia term I learn: supplementation means supplementing breast milk with formula. Because breast is best, as much breast milk as possible should be given, and formula only used to supplement.

I finally break down and give the baby a bottle (she can't drink out of a tequila shot glass forever) and make sure that it is one of the Booby Mafia–approved bottles from England. But once she drinks from a bottle she just won't latch on to me. I call a breast-feeding hotline in a panic and I explain my case: I have one boob, but I'm breast-feeding, but my baby won't suck. Diagnosis: nipple confusion. Duh! My lactation consultant had warned me!

Another lactation consultant squeezes me in for a special visit.

She wants to observe how the baby is behaving and why she isn't latching on. She tells me that I am not allowed to give the baby the bottle for a week. Not even the shot glass. I have to tape a plastic straw (attached to a pack of formula) onto my nipple so whenever the baby sucks my nipple, she gets formula from the plastic straw. If this sounds bizarre, imagine how it looks. I do not shower for three days for fear that I will tape the straw back onto my nipple incorrectly. My wardrobe is limited to Tyler's Tulane sweatshirt, the one that I wore after I had the milk quarts sewn into me for my reconstruction surgery. I am housebound and begin to recognize the Chinese food delivery guys.

I am also instructed to start pumping so that I will keep producing milk, and so that even if Skye does not latch on, I can give her breast milk in a shot glass (or sneak a bottle). The Booby Mafia orders that I pump at least three times a day. The theory goes that if you pump more, you will produce more. But there is one problem: nothing is coming out. Well, something is, but only in drips. Booby Mafia tells me that I am probably using the wrong pump and suggests that I order a more powerful one.

Okay, crank up the horse power because I am going for industrial strength. I am so desperate, I consider putting my boob in my vacuum cleaner. When I see a place called Grandma's in the Yellow Pages I am instantly reassured. When I inquire about the pump the kindly saleswoman, who sounds like a grandma, asks me which model I want and gets very technical.

"Please just bring me the most powerful machine you have."

The industrial-grade pump actually sounds like my vacuum cleaner when I turn it on. It pulls my nipple into a plastic compression chamber and there is quite an impressive spray. But again after hours of churning, only drops. I persevere and watch late night infomercials for hours, the pump and me, just to squeeze out another ounce. Drip by drop.

I keep that vacuum cleaner pump whirring for hours at a time and add up all the drops until there is finally a five-ounce bottle! I am so careful when I transfer the I stayed-up-all-night-to-make-this breast milk into the approved bottle. My daughter slurps and devours that bottle with such abandon that I am sure there are some tears, too, mixed into her next bottle.

After the plastic straw, the vacuum, and a lot of concerned calls from the Booby Mafia, I am exhausted. Almost as exhausted as after a chemo session. They sense it, and as a last-ditch effort not to lose me from their ranks they tell me something I have never heard. I think it is the Booby Mafia Holy Grail: There is a milk bank of other women's breast milk that I can feed my baby from!

Maybe that is the straw that broke this cow's back?

Maybe all this hysteria is really not about milk, ear infections, IQs, or bonding. I think it is really about power. Booby power. Power over men and now power over babies. The power I felt leaving me in the strip club . . . the power I thought I had grabbed back for a moment while I was breast-feeding.

When I see another woman reaching for a bottle of baby formula while I am shopping at the supermarket, I am shocked by how easy it seems. I have been struggling with one boob and machines and contraptions, and in that moment I realize that maybe my first failure as a mother has really become my first success. It would have been so easy if my milk had flowed. Because I worked so hard for those drops, I am convinced that I have been feeding her pure love.

It won't matter if she has a lower IQ and becomes obese because she drinks formula. Forget the breast milk. I've given her an ounce of pure sacrifice and an ounce of pure hope just trying so hard to make up for my missing boob.

I have been trying so hard to be a normal mom to Skye. I think my battle to breast-feed her was just to prove to myself that I could be everything to her and that breast cancer would never come between us. My breast milk did not instantly make me a mom, but my journey to produce it did.

I am her one-boobed mom. And I love her with all of my heart.

Maybe my heart has grown just a little bit bigger to make up for my missing boob?

18

Pushing the
Envelope

I am obsessed with the idea that my cancer is coming back. I feel it growing in the middle of the night. Every time my blood is drawn, my body is scanned, my breast is mammogrammed, my liver is looked at, I am sure they will tell me that I have had a recurrence. Every sore throat, every sore back convinces me that it is cancer. I am living under a cancer cloud.

And to make me even more paranoid, I am working on a story at *20/20* about families who have the breast cancer gene. The more research I do, the more convinced I become that I need to have this gene test for Skye and her future as much as for mine. I've already had breast cancer—so why does a gene matter? A gene will tell me if it can happen again. Not just to me. The stakes are now higher because of Skye.

I can't believe the courage of the women I am speaking with who have the breast cancer gene. The woman we decide to profile, Lori, watched her mother, grandmother, and aunt die from breast cancer, so when she heard there was a gene test, she needed to know. When Lori finds out that she has the gene, she decides to have surgery to remove her healthy breasts and ovaries to try to prevent any chance of getting cancer. Her decision is controversial and some doctors say they would never agree to remove a woman's healthy breasts and ovaries just to make her feel safe. Lori even allows us to follow her into the operating room and to be there after her surgery to ask her if she still feels that she made the right choice.

My mom and her mom did not have breast cancer. My dad's mom didn't. I always thought I didn't have a family history. Breast cancer was one thing our family thought we did not have to worry about, but because I was so young, my doctors think I, too, could have the breast cancer gene. Since I am Jewish, I am at high risk. I have been told that many Jewish women have one of the three common mutations, because not intermarrying has kept breast cancer around.

I am scared to know what my future holds. I am not sure that I want to look in a crystal ball now, because I have had cancer. I am scared that Skye might have the gene, too. I have begun to worry about baby Skye's breasts. Her little pink nipples are so sweet and adorable and I wonder if they might kill her one day.

So I make the ambivalent decision to be tested for the breast cancer gene as a way to make peace with my future. If I have the gene, I will cut off my other breast and cut out my ovaries in a bid to save my life. I will do anything to make sure that I do not have to go through my cancer treatments again. I will cut off anything. That way, maybe I can escape my genetic fate of getting cancer again. Even giving that much away doesn't guarantee I will stay disease-proof. But I will be able to convince myself that I've done everything possible to chase cancer from my life. I am peering into the crystal ball but in the same time hopefully changing it.

It is such an awful decision to have to make, to have another mastectomy and to remove my ovaries, to have to tell Skye that she might have a breast cancer gene so she will worry her whole life. But it is less awful than being diagnosed with cancer again and more chemo.

When I call my parents to ask their advice, they are so sad and guilty and feel somehow responsible for my possible bad gene. I am trying to convince them that their genes gave me their laugh and black hair, but they feel like the gene is their fault. My dad tries to make me laugh when I review the cut-off-everything-so-the-cancer-won't-come-back plan: "Why not cut off your ass while you're at it?"

Truth is, I will cut off anything at this point to make my cancer go away and never come back. When I tell my parents my decision to get the gene test, they surprise me, and tell me that they have already sent their blood to be tested. They knew that I was so terrified and they wanted to take care of it for me. If neither of them have the gene, then I could not have it.

My parents, it turns out, do not have one of the Jewish gene mutations. We are all so relieved! Bur strangely disappointed, too. A gene would have explained why. (Maybe Hallmark should sell a card line: "Congratulations, you don't have the gene." Or "Sorry, I heard you just found out that you have the gene.") But I am not free from genetics yet. My doctors want me to have a more sophis-

ticated test, a breast cancer gene sequence. And I agree. Knowledge is power.

And it's the power of genetics that is seducing me when the
nurse ties a rubber band around my arm to get a vein to bulge. I begin sweating and feeling that blood-drawing nausea that I know
too well from my six months of chemotherapy hell. As I watch the
blood filling the vials, I feel some sort of relief. Could this shiny
red liquid finally unravel the mystery of why I got breast cancer
when I was only twenty-seven years old?

Along with the blood, I must complete a family "pedigree." As
in dogs. The last time I discussed pedigree was when I brought
home my Chesapeake Bay retriever, Jasmine, from a farm. Her
mom was a champion and we had the papers to prove it. I had
never considered my family's pedigree. I have to list all family
members who had cancer, and their relationship to me. I start to
make the list: There was a great-aunt, Mary (my paternal grandpa
Phil's sister, who had breast cancer in her sixties and who died at
eighty-one). There were my dad's second cousins, Ethel and Vicka,
who both now have ovarian cancer—but Ethel is in her seventies,
Vicka in her sixties.

I feel crass for writing their names down, as if they might be
guilty. And I know one day I will become a suspect in my family's
next generation of pedigree. I want to be known as a champion
dog, not just a mutation.

I remember that Aunt Mary was a fiery, rebellious intellectual
who watched her children die of tuberculosis in Russia and then
saw her husband killed because of his political beliefs. She ran an
underground radio broadcast, and despite her years of torture by
the Russian government, she still loved life and was passionate

about cooking and classical music. I thought of Vicka and Ethel—also loud and smart. Ethel is a renowned feminist in Amsterdam, who studied at the Sorbonne. Vicka was a famous musician and writer in Russia, who escaped to America for her freedom.

That is my family's pedigree. That is my bloodline. Feisty, loud-mouthed, smart. Can that be measured in my blood? I want the lab to know that when they look at my blood—can they see *that* through the microscope?

I remember the microscope lady who looked at my blood each time I visited my oncologist. The microscope lady was always wearing her white coat, she never left her white laboratory closet. I passed by her every time I walked by the hallway to see my oncologist. I knew that she was the one responsible for measuring my white counts and looking to see if my tumor markers were up. I didn't know her name. She was always peering into the microscope.

I remember when I saw her at my last visit to my doctor's office, when I brought Skye. Microscope Lady must have been on her lunch break because she was out of her closet and in the hallway. She heard my name called by the nurse and she froze. The baby. She had seen my blood under the microscope for my chemotherapy treatments. She had seen my tumor markers. She had never seen my baby. I saw the tears in her eyes as she rushed past my baby, my biology, and me. And I thought she saw something she had never dreamed possible from inside the microscope: I had survived my cancer. And I had a baby. There will be another microscope lady to look at my six vials of blood that are being FedExed to Salt Lake City. That lady will see one future. I remind myself that I can create another.

But I am obsessed with genes and destiny and I need help. I have seen enough cancer specialists and psychologists and I know I am in trouble when doctors start telling me "You need to see a psychiatrist!" again, about all the gene stuff. Maybe an old-fashioned fortuneteller could calm me down.

I am terrified to hand my over my palm to the psychic. Will she look at my lifeline and see more cancer, more chemotherapy? An early death? I have not had my palm read since my cancer and I really do not want to know what my future holds. Will my cancer come back? If anyone can really see my life ahead of me, what the master plan really is, I'm pretty sure now that I don't want to know it. I don't trust futures anymore.

I reluctantly slide my palm across the table into hers, and then jerk it back. I don't care how good a psychic she is, I don't want any fuck-ups about my lifeline and I don't want her to guess, so I blurt it out. "I had cancer. I found a lump when I was twenty-seven. I'm scared you'll see something strange in my lifeline. Please just don't tell me if it's really bad news. I had a plan, but it went wrong."

The psychic gazes down with her large dark eyes and seduces my hand, with the palm side down. "Honey, you found your lump. Your life is fated."

The psychic then launches into usual-suspect stuff about love and career. But I am not listening at all. She has totally distracted me with the idea that somehow we might be able to have a hand in our fate . . . that our destiny is not in the crystal ball as a pre-set path ahead of us. Is she betraying some psychics' code of honor by telling me this? Or does she really believe that destiny can changed?

The envelope arrives innocently enough with a Land's End catalogue, a mailing from Columbia University asking for money, and an Elmo birthday invitation from one of Skye's friends. The Elmo invitation makes me cry because Elmo is just obliviously happy and I am worried that I have a defective gene.

I am thinking about what the psychic said about my fate when I notice how regular the envelope from the genetic testing lab is. It is bizarre that such life-changing information can just arrive in the mail with an ordinary stamp to deliver it. The envelope is holding my future and I am scared to look. The return address is Myriad Genetic Labs, 320 Wakara Way, Salt Lake City, Utah, and I've not felt such anticipation since opening college admissions packets. But this is a different type of news, not just news about where I might spend the next four years of my life. This news could affect even my great-grandchildren.

I rip open the envelope, and when a pamphlet drops out I know this means trouble. *Testing for Hereditary Cancer Risk: WHAT DOES A "VARIANT OF UNCERTAIN SIGNIFICANCE" MEAN?* I am immediately scared because it is in all caps. This must not be good. Myriad Lab tells me that I have a "genetic variant of uncertain clinical significance." My variant is very serious-sounding: A P1238L. Who comes up with these names, anyway? I read on: "The BRCA1 variant P1238L results in the substitution of leucine for proline at amino acid position 1238 of the BRCAI protein." There is more and more explanation, which, I figure out, explains that they don't know what the hell this means.

I start to cry and then make myself laugh when I say out loud:

"This figures! I'm a mutant mutation." I defy categories. I am caught in a shade of gray for what I thought was an either black or white answer.

Myriad Labs says they have seen this in eleven to twenty-five unrelated families. I suddenly feel a kinship with other P1238Ls, those families out there. Does this mean we are somehow related? Do we all like dim sum and sunsets and talk a lot, all because we share a P1238L?

I start to research my gene. I go onto Medline and e-mail the only researcher in Canada who has published on P1238L. Knowledge is power. He says that he thinks it is insignificant, but he cannot tell me what it means, what my future is.

It takes me awhile to realize that one little P1238L does not a Geralyn make, anyway. If that gene is part of my destiny there are other ones . . . that have not been officially discovered yet. They have to be right around the corner: Scientists in Israel just discovered the "risk-taking" gene called D4DR. I know a scientist somewhere is on the verge of finding the sexy gene. The late gene. The compassionate gene. The funny gene.

And now I know I don't need to wait to open an envelope for my results.

Because as the psychic showed me, I will definitely have a hand in it.

19

Barbie's Boob

I am trying to raise Skye in a boob-proofed universe. But it is impossible: There is a Hooters breastaurant above my therapist's office, and their van always seems to be parked out front. Whenever I watch late-night TV, there are ads for *Girls Gone Wild* videos where college girls lift up their tops and show their boobs for strangers with cameras. And Tyler recently took me to New Orleans and all the women were flashing their breasts at the Mardi Gras parade to get plastic necklace beads. The *Sports Illustrated* swimsuit issue is all over the place, and every bus seems to have a poster with boobs advertising the Victoria's Secret fashion show. Big boobs are definitely in fashion. I am even working on a story at *20/20* about men who conduct business meetings in strip bars, and another story about how breast size influences a woman's personality.

And now Barbie's boobs have entered my home. Skye's Barbie dolls have been pissing me off lately. Their boobs are too big. I never thought I would be the type of mom who would have moral objections to Skye playing with Barbie dolls. I have heard the Barbie-bashing arguments and they are convincing: Real women could never have 39-18-33 figures (that's what Barbie would be if she were human); they would actually fall over. I always wondered how Barbie would walk if she were real—she would have to tiptoe everywhere without her plastic high heels, because her Barbie foot is permanently arched in a 45-degree angle.

I was not mad at Barbie even after I did a story at *20/20* about a woman who decided she wanted to become Barbie and had twenty-seven plastic surgeries to make it happen. But Barbie's boobs were really pissing me off . . . or more precisely, Barbie's *boob*. She has two and I only have one. Hers are so large and are her best feature and mine, I just pray it won't kill me.

I am excited when my sister-in-law Wendy finds a Barbie alternative for Skye on her birthday. Her discovery comes just in time because I was in serious Barbie burn-out mode: For her birthday, Skye received a Barbie car, a Barbie van, a Scooby-Doo Barbie, a Doctor Barbie, a giant Barbie head that talked, and even a Miss Puerto Rico Barbie. Wendy discovered a "Get Real" girl who, unlike Barbie, could actually bend her knees. But the realness did not stop there—the "Get Real" girl could move all of her joints and even came with a surfboard and surf gear. I had grown up playing with girly glitter gowns and matching plastic purses and now I'm asking my daughter to get excited over plastic snow boots and a bendable knee? It seems almost too real to be any fun.

The first thing that Skye does with her "Get Real" girl is rip off her clothing, just like she does with her Barbie dolls. The most striking difference between "Get Real" and Barbie is that "Get Real" girl's breasts are much more real (smaller) than Barbie's. And "Get Real" is wearing a sports-type bra made of plastic that is permanently glued on, compared to Barbie who has two perfect globe-size mounds of plastic.

Skye plays with her "Get Real" girl about three whole minutes and then goes back into Barbie bliss. I don't think she ever touches "Get Real" again, unless I count the time she offered it to her friend Nola because she didn't want to share her Barbie dolls.

Skye prefers her Barbies naked. I think all the interest in her Barbies' boobs has made her interested in mine.

"Mommy, when are you going to get another nipple? Why do you only have one?"

I always wondered how I would explain my breast cancer to Skye. Now she is three, demanding to know why I look different. I don't want her to be scared of her breasts. She is becoming very interested in body parts and even knows what her elbow is. The word *nipple* especially cracks her up, and she giggles and points to herself—"Skye's nipples."

"Mommy had a boo-boo and its name was cancer," I tell her.

Skye loves boo-boos and wants to put a Band-Aid on my boob. She takes her blanket and puts it over my breast and says "Abracadabra" and it's magic because Mommy's boo-boo is all better now. But I am not sure how to explain the one nipple missing, and the tattoo that is there instead. Skye didn't even exist when I first got it. One day, she solves the problem for me: "Mommy's nipple." She points to my left breast and pauses at my right. "And Mommy's cartoon." Cartoons are Skye's obsession, her absolute favorite thing in her little world. Every mommy has two nipples—Skye seems so impressed that hers has a cartoon.

But Skye will soon outgrow cartoons, and she tells me she has a great idea. "Mommy you can tape a nipple on." I will need to explain to her that her breasts might be cancerous one day. How will she feel about being so ambivalent towards her breasts? Boobs are everywhere: wet T-shirt contests, *Playboy*, *Penthouse*, strip clubs, the Booby Mafia, and now even Barbie dolls are not safe. How will Skye feel when she goes through puberty and suddenly boys notice her breasts? Will she always live in fear?

For now, Skye, is besotted by boobs. Especially Barbie's. Since she is probably curious about her own little three-year-old body, Barbie must be something to explore. So naked Barbie goes just about everywhere with us—to the pediatrician's office, to nursery school, and very often out to dinner at swanky New York City restaurants. She causes quite a stir. We often get stares. I think it's because Skye is so cute, until my mother is in town staying with us and looks extremely uncomfortable when I pull Skye's naked Barbies out of my pocketbook and put them on the table at a restaurant one night.

"That's obscene!"

I look down and realize there are three naked Barbie dolls with long blond hair and gigantic boobs on our table. She is right—the naked Barbies do not look like a three-year-old's toys at all. They look like miniature versions of the topless dancers I saw in the strip club. And at that moment I understand why I have felt irritated by Barbie recently. Barbie's boobs are bothering me. The fact that they look so perky and perfect. The fact that they are just so big! There is something about Barbie's boobs that I have to figure out.

I do some research to get to the bottom of Barbie's boobs. They are deliberate. Ruth Handler, her creator, had the radical idea in 1959 that little girls would like to play with a doll that had breasts. Ruth thought it would give them a sense of self-esteem and show them they could be anything when they grew up. Until 1959, little girls played with baby dolls, and most male executives laughed at the idea of a doll with breasts and said that the public would never accept that. But Ruth knew she was onto something, and she did get the last laugh—by inventing Barbie.

No wonder Barbie's boobs have provoked me so much lately. Hers are a deliberate symbol of power. Mine almost killed me.

I am still feeling robbed of that power. Booby power taunts me all the time: On my way to my therapist, passing Hooters, I wonder what they might say to me if I went to apply for a waitressing job. Would I get it if I only had one hooter? Am I hallucinating or do Pamela Lee Anderson's and Anna Nicole Smith's breasts keep getting larger? They all look like Barbie dolls. Britney Spears keeps denying a boob job. Okay, now I am losing it. Having one boob makes me feel like I don't belong. I am not a woman. I guess I feel like that "Get Real" girl that Skye tossed into the corner. This is a breast-obsessed society. It starts when little girls are only three! And it just gets worse. It doesn't matter that I have two Ivy League degrees—I have only one boob.

Something that I think is very strange and sad happened to Ruth Handler, though. The woman who made dolls with breasts was diagnosed with breast cancer and had to have a mastectomy. I think that it is bizarre that the woman who brought so many plastic boobs to the world found herself breastless. Not surprisingly, she went on to launch a plastic prosthetic breast line called "Naturally Me" so that women "could be proud to stick their chests out" after a mastectomy.

But I know it is not so natural to put a plastic mound where your flesh and blood used to be. Plastic boobs—on dolls or real women—feel so hollow. But plastic boobs, even on a doll, are such a powerful toy for a little girl to play with.

I wonder if Ruth herself ever considered making a Breast Cancer Barbie. I mean, they have a Doctor Barbie, Astronaut Barbie, and even a Barbie that does math. If one in eight women get breast cancer, a Breast Cancer Barbie feels more relevant than an astronaut one.

I cannot get the image of Breast Cancer Barbie out of my head. Could Breast Cancer Barbie still somehow be beautiful with a large red bolt across her chest? Maybe if there were a Breast Cancer Barbie, a Hooter Girl, a one-boobed pin-up girl in *Playboy*, a one-boobed stripper, I might find it easier to imagine. I would know there is somehow a template for that beauty.

I have never seen a beautiful woman revealing her boobless-ness, and I cannot summon it up no matter how hard I try. I still cannot look at myself in the mirror. But sometimes, when Tyler and Skye are asleep, I check myself out at 4 A.M. in the shadows of my bedroom. I study the curve of the implant, the bold red diagonal stripe across my chest, and the tattoo at the end of the red line. It is interesting-looking, and the curve even seems natural enough after all that stretching. It is prettier than I expected, in the shadows, in the dark. It looks better than I ever thought it would. When the shadows move across it, my mastectomy looks a little sexy in a really weird way. It is definitely not a breast, but it has its own appeal.

When I get the call from *Self* magazine to pose topless for their breast cancer handbook, the timing feels right. I have just started to look at myself and I want other young women just diagnosed to see a reconstructed boob with a real young woman's head, not just an anonymous torso, because I remember how much the breast mug shots still scare me. Posing would not be about vanity—it would be charity. At least that was what I expected. After all, I had never seen a beautiful woman with just one breast.

20
Developing

"Take off your shirt!"

Okay. Now I am seriously having second thoughts.

I expected some foreplay and I am startled by how forward the photographer is being. This is like jumping into bed with a stranger. I imagined that a topless photo shoot would be more artful than this.

I remind myself why I am here and why this is a special topless photo: I knew I would not end up on any teenager's bedroom wall or locker door. I would not be offered a guest appearance on *Baywatch*, and I am not getting paid big bucks. I agreed to do this because I need to show other women that a mastectomy would not be as horrible as they thought. When the editor at *Self* made the pitch to me to pose topless in the magazine, it sounded so hopeful: "To offer inspiration to other women facing reconstructive surgery after breast cancer."

But I don't think that the way I look could inspire anyone. I just want them not to be scared of what they'll look like. Maybe it will give them a sense of relief that they won't look as bad as they thought they would. The magazine editor told me the photos would be "beautiful" because they had hired a very famous portrait photographer. But I rolled my eyes when she told me over the phone they would be beautiful, because she had not seen what I look like. Let's get one thing straight, I remind myself: This is charity.

I will do anything for breast cancer, but this is extreme. I am being Mother Teresa. Extreme charity. I am so scared that I will be ridiculed and end up on some Internet fetish porn site. I am scared that every ex-boyfriend who broke my heart, every math teacher who gave me a C, will see this and smirk.

I have become a reluctant activist. I will speak to any woman who has just been diagnosed. I do it because of Julie's death. That night I gave my first speech as a breast cancer survivor was the night she died from breast cancer when she was only thirty-four. I need to make sense of her death. My breast surgeon and oncologist give out my number so women can call me. I have met so many women in bathrooms in bars across the city and let them feel me up that it is bordering on slutty. I convinced my breast surgeon and therapist to do the Sally Jessy Raphael show with me. I was worried I might get ambushed and that it might turn into "lingerie after a mastectomy," but it was totally tasteful up until my breast surgeon was asked to do a breast exam live on a model on national television: I know that even though he is a boob doctor, it made him blush. My most outrageous event was "Boarding for Breast Cancer." They flew me out to Heavenly Mountain in California to speak to snowboarders about breast cancer. The event was in memory of a young snowboard-clothing designer, Monica, who died of breast cancer at only twenty-eight. I had to go, of course, because it could have been me who had died at twenty-eight. I did not expect that I would have to speak to a crowd of nearly five hundred rowdy teenagers (mostly male) about breast cancer. It was a tough sell, especially because I had to speak after the Foo Fighters performed. The crowd looked like they might start heckling me at any second. I was not wearing the right thing. I had to be strategic and win over my audience. At the top of my lungs I screamed into the microphone, "Touch yourself!"

The crowd roared. Earlier in the day I had seen a few snowboarders wearing T-shirts with that slogan. I kept going. "You all have dirty minds. I was talking about breast self-exams. And guys, you should learn how to do it, too. It's quite a pick-up line and so many lumps are found by women's boyfriends."

I told my story—how I had touched myself and saved my life. There was silence. When I finished, someone started chanting: "Touch yourself! Touch yourself!"

Some really hot young guys carried me off stage, and the crowd was still screaming.

But now in the taxi heading downtown to the photographer's chic Noho studio to have my topless photo taken, this feels more daring than facing a crowd of hecklers. I keep reminding myself of how many women I am going to help. I am trying hard to remember looking at my plastic surgeon's breast photo book—the breast mug shots, the headless torsos. I know that attaching a head to a torso with a mastectomy, especially a young one, will be so helpful, because I receive so many calls from recently diagnosed women who want to see what my reconstruction actually looks like, who got my name from friends, family, and my doctors. I know how important it is to take this picture because I have seen the relief in their eyes when I unfastened my bra in the bathrooms across the city.

I remember what I imagined I might look like after my mastectomy, and I imagined horrible things. I always make sure to wear my best push-up bra when I meet these women, and even let them feel the reconstructed breast if they want to. I tell them how great I think I look, but part of me feels like I am lying. I need to reassure them. It is an incredible show-and-tell. They are so relieved to actually see me instead of the breast mug shots/headless torsos in the photo book. I know taking this photograph will be important. I need to put a head with a boob for all those young women.

I'm only a few blocks away and I start to panic: What if a woman looks at me and is supposed to feel inspired but really feels appalled? What if I scare her? I feel like I'm opening a door for someone to see what is behind it. I can almost taste their disappointment. I consider going back uptown. Instead I am an hour late.

I think maybe I'm in the wrong place when I walk into the bland entranceway and enter the creaky freight elevator with the big iron gate, because it is not glamorous. But when the elevator jumps to a stop at the ninth floor I know I am at the right place—when I step out of the elevator, I smell how hip the place is. Incense, perfume, photography chemicals, and air conditioning are blending together to create some sort of tonic that instantly reassures me I am in a famous photographer's studio.

I am unsure of how to introduce myself to such a famous photographer—does she even care what my name is? It's sort of that feeling you get when you introduce yourself to your new gynecologist. She just wants to look. I am the one-boobed poster girl. This famous photographer usually photographs celebrities—strictly A-list, no B's. What am I?

I had done a Google search on the famous photographer before my session, and I was thoroughly impressed. She has traveled across America and captured bizarre and disturbing images in the heartland. One of her most famous shots is of a little girl smoking in her plastic kiddy pool. The picture is pretty incredible because she actually got the rings of smoke, and the way this little girl is standing, she looks so mature. But then you see her pudgy thighs sticking out of a frilly bathing suit and remember that she is only eight, and how could her mother let her smoke a cigarette? This is good photography. She has even had fellowships named after her, and exhibitions in Venice and Barcelona, and her work starts conservatively at ten grand.

Then I notice something that terrifies me. There are a lot of stylists for this shoot: hair, makeup, and wardrobe. Good-looking, cool young guys standing around, kind of slouching, posing, looking bored, but snapping to attention whenever she needs something. Are they going to be in the room? Will they see my scar, too? I have no problem with the camera, the photographer, and other breast cancer patients seeing it, but these guys? I mean, they seem sweet, but I don't want them to look at me without my shirt on. Should I ask them to leave? But is that totally hypocritical to show my boobs to thousands of strangers and care that a few people will see them first? I don't want to make waves before I take off my shirt. I want them to like me before they need to see me.

I watch her moving around her studio, commanding it in a very synchronized fashion while taking the picture of a woman before me. There is a lot of commotion as she adjusts her light and lens, and then she takes some deep breaths. There is absolute silence before the loud, crackling, flashbulb *pop*. It is as if she is capturing the image in her net, like a butterfly.

An assistant ushers me over to the buffet while the photographer is finishing her last photo. The buffet is magnificent. There are little signs that explain the food in detail: free-range chicken salad with basmati rice and organic beets and basil vinaigrette. Maybe this is why women pose topless? I am excited to dig in, but the now anxious assistant tells me, "Sorry, you can't eat now because she is ready for you." I am led across the large loft, and everyone parts like the Red Sea.

I don't know what I think should come next but I am stunned. Just "Take off your shirt." I don't know how I thought I would actually remove my shirt. Maybe I thought that they would wrap me in a cloak like those art school nude models, and suddenly the gown would fall to the floor in a dramatic whoosh. The assistants don't give me a gown and they are not leaving the room. She tells me to stand on a platform. And she is waiting for me to take off my shirt.

I am tugging on my T-shirt to stall while deciding if I should play along and be cool or ask everyone to leave except her and the *camera*. I am trying hard to be blasé: So what that I am posing topless even though I only have one boob? But I am a lot more scared than I thought I was going to be. I start to sweat and that's when I panic, because I remember that I have not worn deodorant—I was scared a white ring might show under my armpit in the picture.

I realize how ridiculous it is that I chose to wear a foxy bra. It does not matter. It's boob time. I am fumbling with my bra strap and I look up and that's when I meet her eyes for the first time. She seems to be getting impatient with me and I feel like a melon waiting to be examined in the produce section.

I am still fumbling with my bra and there is still a small crowd just waiting to see what I look like. I am terrified to unhook my bra around all these cool people. I am chickening out. One of them approaches me with a can of hair spray and a blow dryer to break the tension and fix my hair, which is now messy from pulling my T-shirt so sharply over my head. She glares at him and turns her attention to me. She instantly starts seducing me. She tells me that I look perfect. She is a flirt—it is hard to say no to her.

"Don't touch her hair. I love it wild like that."

Someone in the small crowd tells her he has not done my makeup and another says he has not even touched my hair. She doesn't care. She wants my bra off. Now.

What is she thinking? I didn't even brush my hair this morning because they told me they would have "hair and makeup" at the shoot. My hair is the authentic bed-head look and I am craving some lipstick. I ask her if I could have some lipstick, please, pretty please, I need lipstick. I need something to center me here. I need to lick that beeswax and taste the courage.

"Give her some lipstick!"

This is more like it. But she will only indulge me so long and she starts to sigh and I know the bra has to come off.

I want this famous photographer to like me. I want to be cool. I don't want it to seem like a big deal. But it is. Forget my messy hair and that I need makeup—I need a nipple. I am fretting that my reconstructed mastectomy-side breast is so much higher than the other real one, there is no symmetry. I can hide it with bras that have underwire and smush them up so there is an illusion that things are working, but there is nowhere to hide here under the bright lights that she is instructing another assistant to adjust.

I keep breathing and take off the bra.

Breathe. Look up.

Breathe. Look down.

Breathe. I see my tattoo and I smile, but I do wish for maybe a second that I had gotten a nipple. I could really use a nipple at a time like this.

She walks over to me and tells me to put my hands on my hips.

"What?"

Maybe I am naïve but I thought she was going to put me in some artistic pose where you couldn't really see a full frontal . . . maybe an arm draped gracefully across my chest so you couldn't tell I'm missing my right nipple, or maybe I would cup my hands under my breasts so they would be slightly covered?

"Can't I just drape my arm over my chest?" Now I am begging.

"No. Everyone will wonder what you're hiding. Put your hands on your hips!"

I must have completely tensed my body because she yells, "Stop!" and has to reposition my hands. I am such a loser that I cannot even put my hands on my hips correctly. I start sweating more. The men are now very close, hovering and inspecting my hands to make sure they are right. Do I smell? I could have used my husband's deodorant because it's a clear stick, to avoid deodorant lines in my topless photo. Do they airbrush out deodorant lines? Can they airbrush in a nipple?

When I look around everyone is still gathered about the photographer and waiting. They have seen my chest. They are slouching as if to show they don't care, but they must be horrified. They are pretending not to notice me, which is making it worse. I don't know what I expect them to say. I'd be relieved if they were thinking "It doesn't look as bad as we thought it would." Every time she moves they are anticipating her reactions and ready to lurch.

She positions me on a platform in front of the camera. There is complete silence in the room as she steps behind her camera.

It is a camera that perfectly matches her. It is spectacular. Grand. I have never seen a camera so big. It must be six feet long and three feet wide. It looks old-fashioned and makes a lot of noises. One of the articles I read said that she takes pictures with this camera and that there are only three in the country! I picture her driving across the Midwest with the camera in its own car. On the front of the camera is the word *Polaroid*, and it is not until I look up at the photo on the wall that I realize what Polaroid means. As in instant picture. The photo is almost billboard size, black and white, of course (she only photographs in black and white). It is of a young woman who did not have reconstruction and she seems so brave and proud of herself. I have never seen such large pictures—they are imposing and humongous. I am not that brave. I cannot have this picture taken. I am wondering how large my scar will look blown up on a billboard as I hear the momentary silence and see stars from the flash of white light. The white flash reminds me of the operating room lights and I have the same strange dizzy sensation that I felt when they put me to sleep before my surgeries. I lick my lipstick for strength.

It takes about six minutes for the camera to spit out the picture. I am standing on the platform covering myself with a shirt someone has brought over to me. I have not put it on, I am just holding it up. There is lots of gurgling, and the mood in the room feels clouded with the tension of waiting. There is only whispering so as not to disturb her.

I cannot help but feel dread. I am so scared that this picture will be awful. Now I have almost forgotten my motivation for being charitable. Now I am only vain. Just waiting for a billboard-sized me with no "hair and makeup," no nipple, no beauty.

I stare up at the white emptiness waiting for myself to appear. I am waiting for the reaction of the men in the room, too. I know that they will all be disappointed.

I am thinking this will be the same disappointment I've felt seeing every picture ever taken of me, but even worse. Either my nose looked crooked or my teeth were too big or I hated my outfit. I remember my second grade school picture. My hair was knotted and I was wearing a hand-me-down yellow shirt with an elephant that was awful. In my high school graduation picture my bangs looked like a helmet and my cheeks were chubby. I had given up on liking my image. Somehow I always thought I looked better than the picture showed. Photos betrayed me. People would console me by saying, "You're much prettier in person."

Everyone follows her to the wall. Two of them climb a ladder and take clothespins to fasten the eight-foot version of me on the wall. I cannot watch. I am still posed on the platform holding my hands on my hips the way she had instructed. I think I might vomit. When I do glance up the paper is blank, and everyone is holding their breath as the image is revealing itself, developing in chunks of gray, black, and white before them.

Suddenly, the mood has changed as if a breeze had blown through the studio. She is giddy. So everyone is happy. I have to look over to see what the commotion is. Has someone told a joke?

They are smiling and standing around in a semi-circle. They are all huddled around the eight-foot version of me.

I take a peek and I am tempted to see more. To give scale perspective, my belly button is about the size of a silver dollar. I walk towards the crowd and overhear snippets: "Strong. Jawbone—fabulous." "Fantastic cheeks."

I am waiting to hear what they say about the huge three-foot-wide scar, the off-center mound, the missing nipple, the obvious flaws of the photo.

I can't look . . . not yet. I need to speak to her first. I have changed my mind and can't allow this picture to be published. I will make her burn it—I will pay her $10,000 if I have to.

I pull her aside and I mumble, stutter, for the first time in my life. "I can't do this. I'm sorry. I thought when I agreed to be in the magazine that I might be able to cover my mastectomy scar a little more. I am so mortified. I'm scared for other women to see my wound. They'll be scared. This is all wrong."

She looks confused. Have I insulted her?

"LOOK AT YOURSELF! You look so"—pause—"ballsy! My God. It's so powerful."

I tell her I'm scared to look. I start to cry. I squint up and gulp in my humiliation. The men in the room are handsome and I suddenly realize how revealed I am. I have spent so much time in front of the mirror trying to conceal the missing breast. I found the right bras, the right shirts. I even have cleavage. I can pass. No one has known what I really look like underneath it all. I have only allowed myself to look in the shadows at night. That scar. My wound.

I remember how scared I had been to first look at myself after surgery. Dr. B had made me. I remember how scared I had been to look at my new tattooed nipple. Josh made me. I had accepted those moments as small victories, but they did not sustain.

This was the first time I would see myself in a photo, and it was eight feet tall. This is the first time I would see my new body with no cover-ups and hiding. When I finally look I cover one eye.

I don't recognize myself. I see my eyes and a depth I have never seen before. I see a journey. My eyes are telling me that I can look now. I can see me. What has developed on that paper is different than what I had ever imagined myself to be.

I am face to face with an eight-foot, black-and-white version of myself, at first unfamiliar, until she convinces me that it is me. The camera does not lie. There are no judgments, no voices, no wishes, no more what I wanted to be. There I am—no hiding, no posing, no touch-ups, no giggles, no sorrys, no sunglasses, no excuses, no mojo, no baseball caps, no wigs, no comparisons, no push-up bra that makes me look normal, no time to get angry . . .

I see my lipstick. It is ironic that my lipstick and the scar are the same color red. The black and white photo does not show this, but I know.

I remember the first time I wore it, when I thought only movie stars could really pull it off. This lipstick is not about glamour. I do deserve to wear it, though. I remember putting on the lipstick before being wheeled into my surgery. I remember how hopeful I wanted the lipstick to be, to remind me of a life that might await me. I remember when I had stopped wearing lipstick because no one was looking anyway. Maybe now, it is just for me. I remember how I hoped I would wear lipstick again on my own terms. Now I have, and for the whole world to see.

I am not the same. I have definitely changed. I see one breast that nursed a baby, and one breast that nearly killed me. It is this contradiction that has vexed me: life and death are both so close to my heart now.

My scar looks like a skid mark, where I hit the brakes and came so close to death. I want to finally accept it while it is in front of me, blown up in black and white. It is revealing my pain for everyone to see and there is no hiding.

This famous photographer has worked her magic. She has captured the courage that was mingled with my fear and turned out a beauty so honest and raw it is unfamiliar. She has convinced me that maybe I have never really seen myself. The new me.

In the photo my scar is a powerful bolt of a line, but only one piece of a mosaic. How could it be only that and not the whole focus of the photo? I remember the picture she took of the little girl smoking in her wading pool. I know now why she is famous.

I never existed as a beautiful woman until I saw myself that July day in her chic Noho studio. In every photo in the past I hated my nose, my cheeks, my smile. Now, when there is a huge defect, I was the most beautiful.

I had set out to inspire other women that they could be beautiful after this surgery and I ended up convincing myself.

The wonder of that moment dissipates pretty quickly the moment the magazine actually hits the newsstands. I stay in bed for a day and worry about every ex-boyfriend, every teacher, and every boss who might see my nudie picture. I worry that they will see my defect, but I worry more about all the women I was supposed to inspire.

She answers my question just when I thought I had done the wrong thing. Her e-mail tells me that she is just twenty-eight, and when her breast surgeon told her that she had cancer and she needed a mastectomy she fled his office. She happened to stop at a newsstand on her way home. She happened to buy that issue of *Self* magazine. When she got home she saw my picture. She knew she could do it after she saw me. I hadn't scared her.

I got a call from another young woman. She said my picture was displayed on her coffee table. The only other time I had heard of displaying breasts on coffee tables was when my uncle kept his Marilyn Monroe book on display in his beach house. But my breasts? She told me she had breast cancer, and she had brought my picture to her doctor appointments and showed all of her friends. She wanted to look just like me.

Even though I wanted to inspire those young women, in the end it turned out not to be about inspiring anyone else. I finally accepted myself.

It has taken more than my surgery to build the perfect boob. And I realize it actually isn't about my boob or my scar, my hair, my nipple, or any of that. The camera has captured a me I never knew I could become. Somehow I have developed in front of my own eyes.

I remember my journey . . . where it began in the strip bar. I was so scared I would never be the same again without my boob. And I am not. I remember how I sat in the strip bar feeling the power draining out of me. I remember the stripper. I remember her swagger, and how it really wasn't about her boobs. It was about her attitude and how even though she was giving so much away, she still was holding on to herself so fiercely that it was hot. It was powerful.

I have posed topless for millions to see me with just one boob. I have given away so much, but I feel more powerful than I ever did before, even with my two boobs. How can I be most beautiful when I had lost the most?

How do I explain this irony?

I have finally learned how to strip.

Afterword: The Sky's the Limit: All the Places I Have Worn Lipstick

It is amazing, all the places where I have worn my lipstick. Places I never dreamed I would be on the morning of my mastectomy. I wore lipstick to the White House to meet the President while on assignment for Lifetime Television, to Skye's first day of preschool and to her kindergarten interviews. I wore lipstick to my brother Howard's wedding, and when I first held his daughter, Stella, in my arms. I wore lipstick to my mother's sixtieth birthday, and my father's sixty-fifth. I was wearing lipstick when I heard Paul made partner. I got lipstick all over Tyler when I kissed him on our ten-year wedding anniversary in St. Thomas, under the stars.

And there are so many places I still want to wear lipstick to:

Skye's college graduation, her wedding. I want to live to watch Skye wear lipstick. Actually, I want to be one of those hunched over old, old ladies who wears bright red lipstick.

Sometimes I think about what would have happened if I had not done that breast exam and saved my life. All the moments and all the lipstick shades I would have missed.

I still think of all the women I have met who will never get to wear lipstick. Their beautiful faces and their dreams keep me up at night.

It was hard to imagine that I could ever wear lipstick again: I was scared that the other lipstick moments would not live up to my defining lipstick moment. Just wearing lipstick to drink a cup of coffee, go to work, go out to the movies. But maybe that is what is so special about them now—they are so ordinary. I have gotten my life back, and each moment I'm living feels especially lipstick-worthy.

But there is a strange lipsticky residue from that day that I have never been able to wipe from my lips. Each time I put it on is a moment of reflection, of appreciation that I am not in the hospital or sick from cancer treatments. I am so free without my IV line.

Each time I wear lipstick, I am emboldened by the memory of that day: the IV line in my arm, my surgical gown on with my butt hanging out, and my perfectly applied lipstick.

I swear I can still taste that hope.

Geralyn's Favorite Breast Cancer Resources

1. Anastacia Fund
bcrfcure.org

Listen to the beauty and the power of the singer/songwriter Anastacia's voice if you need to feel inspired. Anastacia is raising awareness through funds that specifically target younger women who get breast cancer and have no family history of the disease. The Anastacia Fund is run through The Breast Cancer Research Foundation, founded in 1993 by Evelyn H. Lauder of The Estée Lauder Companies.

Donations:
The Anastacia Fund—BCRF
Suite 1209
654 Madison Avenue
New York, NY 10021

2. Big Bam!
Bigbam.com

Janice Bonadio was only twenty-seven, the same age that I was, when she found a lump in her breast. She was diagnosed with breast cancer and had no health insurance. She realized that she could make a huge difference by serving women like herself, and started The Big Bam!, an organization committed to reaching under-served women. They provide free self-exam cards, and host free mammogram screenings. Janice is now changing the world: "It scares me to know that most women in their twenties feel they are too young to have to do a breast self-exam or simply don't know how to do it; and that there are so many uninsured women who cannot afford a mammogram. I had to do something to change this."

Donations:
The Big Bam!
51 MacDougal Street
Suite 487
New York, NY 10012

3. Breast cancer.org
breastcancer.org

I had to get nine consults and go on Medline to figure out my treatment options. If only I had had breastcancer.org, founded by Dr. Marisa Weiss, a compassionate and brilliant oncologist who wants to empower women by helping them understand their medical choices. Women's questions about treatment are answered 24/7 with the most reliable, complete, and up-to-date information about breast cancer available, allowing patients to make the best decisions about their treatment.

Dr. Weis also wrote *Living Beyond Breast Cancer: A Survivor's Guide for When Treatment Ends and The Rest of Your Life Begins*, because there is a different "normal" after cancer happens.

Donations:
breastcancer.org gifts
111 Forrest Avenue 1R
Narberth, PA 19072

4. B4BC
b4bc.org

Boarding for Breast Cancer (B4BC) was started by a group of women to honor their friend who died from breast cancer when she was only twenty-nine, largely because she was misdiagnosed and told she was "too young" for the disease. These cool snowboarding chicks reach young women with music and sports to let them know that you are never too young to have breast cancer. What a beautiful tribute to a friend!

Donations:
Boarding for Breast Cancer Foundation
6230 Wilshire Blvd #179
Los Angeles, CA 90048

5. Dr. Sandra Haber
drhaber.com

Dr. Haber is a talented psychologist who specializes in treating cancer patients and their families. What a lifesaver.

6. Lifetime Television (Stop Breast Cancer for Life 10-Year Anniversary)
lifetimetv.com

One reason I work at Lifetime Television is their passion to stop breast cancer. Check out their awareness campaign and the amazing programming they do each October to create awareness and offer hope.

7. *Self* Magazine
selfmagazine.com

Check out the *Self* Breast Cancer Handbook in October. *Self* magazine cares about women all year round, too, and is celebrating it twenty-fifth anniversary of making a difference in womens' lives. To subscribe, go to selfmagazine.com.

8. Young Survival Coalition
youngsurvival.org

You are not alone! There is a community of young survivors waiting to talk to you about your fertility, your treatment options, and dating. I wish this group had existed when I was diagnosed! The Young Survival Coalition was started in 1998 by three young breast cancer survivors who were all under the age of thirty-five at diagnosis. They felt discouraged by the lack of information and resources available to young women, and are concerned about the under-representation of young women in breast cancer studies.

Donations:
The Young Survival Coalition
52A Carmine Street
Box 528
New York, NY 10014

9. Zeta Tau Alpha
zetataualpha.org

Even college women are now aware of the risks of breast cancer, largely due to the Zeta Tau Alphas. They have made their national philanthropy cause breast cancer awareness and education. Get involved on college campuses. And "Think Pink!"

Special Thanks

I am profoundly grateful to everyone who believed in this project and supported me in my journey to tell my story.

Jennifer Weis believed passionately in this project from the moment Meredith White told her that I was writing this book. Jennifer, thank you for believing in this book, and thank you for your wisdom in showing me exactly what I needed to include (especially sex with my bandages on)! I feel very close to you after sharing so much!

Elizabeth Beier blew me away when we first met by noticing that I was wearing chandelier earrings like the ones I wore after my mastectomy surgery. Thanks for your support, too.

I feel a little like J Lo talking about my agent, Joelle delBourgo, and bringing her with me to all my meetings, but every woman needs Joelle by her side. You are so tenacious! Thank you for believing in this project and for seeing how it could really reach women. Thank you for being so devoted and dedicated and always wearing lipstick! (Elan, thanks for all of your help!) Caryn Karmatz-Rudy was an early fan of this project, and I am very appreciative of her huge vote of confidence. . . . Caryn's confidence goes a long way. My lawyers, Conrad Rippy and Kim Schefler Rodriguez, made hard conversations easy with their incredible brains.

There were many amazing writing classmates who read almost every incarnation of every chapter of this book: thank you to Corey, Lillian, Christopher, Eve, Judith, Jo Ann, and recently, Sabrina and Nina. And, to our professor, Janet Flora, thank you for believing in me more than I believed in myself. Thank you for being so incredibly supportive and for all of your fabulous ideas about writing. Thank you for reading every draft of this book and being so enthusiastic about each one. I hear your voice whispering in my ear whenever I write now. Your voice helped me to find mine. (Also, a special thanks to Karol Nelson, my first Gotham teacher, and Judith Crist, my Columbia "Personal Style" professor.) Lorrie Bodger not only did an amazing line edit, she took all the pieces everyone else had helped me to compile and figured out how they fit together, what repeated, and what was missing. Lorrie took all of the ingredients and made a gourmet meal (she writes cookbooks, too!), and she did it under a huge deadline. Lorrie was always true to my vision of the book and kept my voice intact while smoothing out my edges.

I need to thank some amazing women at *Self* magazine for being the first to tell my story and to make me think that I had a story to tell. I need to thank *Self* for being so devoted to women's lives and so devoted to ending breast cancer, long before it was the chic thing to do. Because it was the right thing to do. Rochelle Udell did my first story in *Self* about my crewcut hair after my chemo. Rochelle also did the story about the circle of friends who supported me, and had the idea to take a picture of me when I was the largest I've ever been in my life, days away from giving birth to my daughter, Skye. The caption on the photo was "Survivor Pride." That was being kind—it was more like "Wide Load," but I never felt more lucky to be a wide load show other women that they, too, might be lucky enough to have a baby after breast cancer. Rochelle is a visionary in communicating important things to women. Rochelle has been there on many other levels—she came to the hospital to hold Skye when she was born. Rochelle, I treasure our friendship. Lucy Danziger arranged for me to have my topless photo taken for *Self* to show my reconstruction to other young women. The first chapter I ever wrote was about that photo. That experience inspired me to tell my story. When I told Lucy about my experience writing that chapter, she told me that I had to write a book, and that *Self* would support it. Well, of course, Lucy went all out in her Lucy way. *Self* is running the first serial and continues to support me. Donna Fennesey has done an incredible job with the serial, and is always incredible. Dana Points has also been wonderful. Beth Brenner has been a constant friend and supporter. Thank you!

I need to thank some incredible women who told my story before I could even tell my story: Donna Murphy and Porter Gayle. (My cousin, Mira, introduced me to these dynamos: thanks, Mira!) Donna and Porter (A.K.A. 2 Chicks of the 2 Chicks, 2 Bikes, 1 Cause) road their bikes across the country to create awareness about young women and breast cancer. Donna and Porter are very strong (their emotions and their biceps), and sharing my story with them helped me to share my story now.

Julie Huang and Erika Angulo told my story for their Columbia University journalism master's project. Peter Herford was their advisor and my advisor, therefore, the project was incredibly meaningful. Even though they were only journalism students, their professionalism, sensitivity, and intelligence were scary.

I also need to thank the professional supporters I have had in my life. My colleagues at *20/20* became friends during this hell. They were all cool, supportive, and always showed me that my brain was still okay while everything else was falling apart. Victor Neufeld, David Tabacoff, and Meredith White promoted me and gave me a contract during my chemo, when I was scared I was going to die. It was a huge vote of confidence. Barbara Walters sent me the most insane flowers after my surgeries! She even gave flowers to my parents! So many other incredibly supportive people were there when I was going through treatments: Allan Maraynes, Jamie Zahn, Joe Pfifferling, Alan Goldberg, David Sloan, Carla De-Landri, Katie Thompson, Nola Safro, Mia Walker, Eric Neuhaus, Julia Eisenman, Patricia Arico. . . .

And, my colleagues at Lifetime Television who have been so supportive: Allison Wallach, Alysa Hangtan, Liz Gateley, Claudine Battisti, Emily Harrold, Toby Graff, Carole Black, Meredith Wagner, Elise McVeigh, Barbara Brennan, Marianne Goode, Robin Palmer, Denise Farrell Young, and, especially Mary Dixon. Mary Dixon and I have started a special tradition: every year, to celebrate our diagnosis anniversary, we drink champagne for breakfast. Mary is a constant support system to me and I am proud to call her my friend. Lifetime has featured me in their "Stop Breast Cancer for Life" campaign, and has always made me feel that being a survivor was something that I could be proud of at work, and never, ever had to hide. That is pretty powerful!

So many people have been dedicated to getting this book out there . . . thank you!

At St. Martin's: Steve Snider, Matt Baldacci, Carrie Hamilton-Jones, Sally Richardson, Stefanie Lindskog, Steve Cohen, Caroline Gregorio, Paul Sleven, and Courtney Fischer.

At Lifetime TV: Mary Dixon, Meredith Wagner, Carole Black, Kim Bogosian, Marian Effinger, Norris Post, Kris Soumas, Denise Farrell Young, Todd Unger, Lisa Black, Allison Wallach, Bill Brand, and Elise McVeigh

At Betsey Johnson: Catherine Nation, Agatha Szczepaniak, Betsey and Ali Froley

At Young Survival Coalition: Michelle Przypyszny and Cindy Rubin

At Breast Cancer Research Foundation: Myra Biblowit, Anna DeLuca, Robbie Finke, and Pat Altman

At Lauder: Evelyn Lauder and Sally Susman

At Stila: Carineh Martin, Kate Hall, and Jacqui Tractenberg

At B4BC: Justine Chiara

At Big Bam: Janice Bonadio

At breastcancer.org: Marisa Weiss and Hope Wohl

At *Self*: Cheryl Marker, Lauren Theodore, Dana DeVito, Beth Brenner, Lucy Danziger, Donna Fannesey, and Dana Points

At Zeta Tau Alpha: Nicole Patterson and Sherry Tilley

Of course I could not have written this book (or survived my ordeal) without an incredible personal support system.

Tyler gets special thanks. Tyler was brave enough to let me write openly and honestly about our relationship. Pretty impressive. Actually, if the tables were turned, I'm not sure I would have allowed that. I mean it. Think about how generous he is to have exposed himself—or rather let me expose him—in this way. Wow. I hope the overall impression that comes across about Tyler is that he was deeply in love with his wife, but scared shitless about what was happening. I hope the overall impression is that of the loving and caring, but worried husband that he was. Tyler, by letting me be honest about us, I think we will help other people be honest about their situations. You were my knight in surgeon's scrubs. I think your surgeon's scrubs, ironically, actually made you feel helpless. Thank you for loving me. Thank you for supporting me in writing this book. Thank you for making me a mom. Thank you for all the nights you watched Skye while I was writing. Skye gets the next thanks. Last week Skye told me that she was going to call 911 if I did not hit "save" on my computer. I know she missed me a lot when I was writing, and I will tell her when she is older that this book is for her. I want her to understand what I lived through and how special and precious her life is to me. That I never take a second of our togetherness for granted. (Hawa and Jen: thank you for always being there for Skye.)

My parents and brothers' love is something I always counted on, but I never knew how much I needed it during my cancer. Harvey and Barbara Weiner: I love and adore you! Thank you for letting me write about what we all went through. Paul and Howard, your support was felt greatly by me. I know that no matter what happens, I will always have your love and support. You are the best brothers and I am a lucky girl. Thank you to Lori and Cheri, too, for all of your love. My extended family was so much a part of my support system, too. My in-laws: Marie, Gerald, Wendy, Leslie, Tom, and Jan. Stephen, Eric, Edi, Alissa Adler, Pamela Murphy, Marilyn and Larry Lindberg, Marty, Andi and Suzanne Weiner, the Kay Family (David, Mira, Brielle, Rebecca, Steve, Rhonda, and Robbi), Honey and Barb, the Myles Girls (Hallie, Lynda, and Wendy), the Portnoys (Bernard and Nancy), and Carol Kohn.

So many people helped me to put my life back together again and made such a huge difference in my life. There was so much you could not read about: my best friends from childhood, Jane Andrews and Diane Zweiman. Thank you for being there for me (along with Robin) since I was three years old! Thank you to the Ratner, Zweiman, and Andrew families, too, for all of their support. Ethan Prochnick went with me to almost every doctor appointment while he was writing a screenplay. How do I ever adequately say "thank you" to Steve Brower, Nancy Napier, Josh Lord, Forrest Murray, Jen Altman, Rebecca and Judy Porter, Suzanne Seltzer, Jessie and Julie Cohen, Robin Sias, Pamela Meisel, Carlin Vickery, the Shapiro Family (Dan, Ellen, Andrew, Peter, Stu Blumberg), Laura Van Straten, Georgia Witkin, Leslie Hurtig, the Altman Family (Jane, Bob, and Jon), Sandra Haber, David Weinstein, Anne Moore, Mary Ellen Mark, Jill Fishbane-Mayer, Andy Liebowitz, Howard Rosenberg, Kevin Fox, Marianne Brower, Shelly and Diana Jacobsen, Robin and Rich Tedesco, Ira, Barbara, and Jesse Schreck. You all were my 18 Hour support bra!

Okay, I saved the best for last. The survivors. Tami Agassi, Leslie Monsky, and Stacey Sager have been so supportive of me telling my story. Melissa Banks called me because our moms had mutual friends and she wanted me to believe that I could live. Thank you!

I want to especially thank three special survivors who paved my way. I need to start with "Aunt" Rena. Rena, you called me because your nephew asked you to. I was a stranger but you became my confidante and mentor and even my "aunt" during this ordeal. You showed me that I could survive, even thrive, after breast cancer. You showed me that every day should be a celebration.

Meredith White, you showed me that I could live again. I wish that every woman could have a "Meredith" while going through breast cancer: a friend, a champion, and an inspiration. I hope that my daughter, Skye Meredith, grows up to be at least half the woman you are. You came to the wig shop, you bought me a sexy bra for my newly reconstructed boobs, and you helped me come out about my cancer at work. And, you made this book happen!

Jane Altman, thank you for teaching me how to be my own best advocate. Thank you for your beautiful daughter, my amazing best friend, Jen. You are both such true friends.

I am humbled by everyone's love and support. . . .